Moving On and Moving Up
In the Marketplace

Practical Principles for Reclaiming
the Seven Mountains of Culture

Naomi Dowdy

Published by
Naomi Dowdy Ministries
P.O. Box 703686 Dallas Texas 75370

ISBN: 978-1-934201-07-7

Printed in Singapore
5 4 3 2 1 08 09 10 11 12

Contents

Preface

This is a wake-up call. It is time to open our eyes and see what is going on in our world today. No, I am not referring simply to the economic crisis, food crisis or oil crisis. I am talking about men and women like yourself whom God has chosen and positioned to make a dynamic impact in our world today.

Everywhere I look, I see God moving His people — perhaps even you — to the next level. He is advancing our understanding of our calling and anointing, enlarging our vision, and preparing us for greater influence and expansion than we have ever imagined. He is doing this so His Kingdom can be established in every sphere of every nation on earth.

I sense in particular that God is moving His marketplace leaders to the next level. He is renewing our minds and changing our mindsets about what our divine assignment really is.

Tom Phillips, who is associated with the Billy Graham Evangelistic Association, said this: "The greatest potential ministry in the world today is in the marketplace. Christ's greatest labor force is those men and women already in that environment." That statement proclaims a powerful message that each one of us needs to grasp.

It is imperative for each of us to know why God has placed us in our particular line of work or business, and connected us with significant leaders in our field. Surely, there must be more to it than just doing business and earning a profit.

However, to discover what God wants to do will require us to first begin to see Scripture differently. It will mean that we must understand ministry differently. We must hear Jesus when He said, "Open your eyes and look at the fields! They are ripe for harvest" (John 4:35b). I believe that God is calling us to embrace again the biblical pattern of ministry.

The model we see in the Bible is that of Jesus going out into society and calling or selecting leaders who were already strategically positioned in the marketplace. There are examples from the Old Testament and also from the New Testament. When the Holy Spirit moved upon their hearts, many of them did not leave their business to 'serve God'. Rather, they served God while they continued to conduct their business. This is the same model that we need to embrace today.

> *They served God while they continued to conduct their business.*

Let me ask you a few questions:
- Are you struggling with what God is calling you to do in the marketplace?
- Do you have a desire to be involved in the marketplace but wonder where you fit?
- Do you sense a stirring in you to do something significant for God through your work or business?

- Do you find yourself procrastinating because you are not sure how to move up to the next level?
- Are you grappling with the changes that might be required of you?
- Do you feel as though you run into walls of opposition or dead ends?
- Are you looking for a business model that would give you a jumpstart?

If you have answered "yes" to any of these questions, it is highly probable that God is moving you up to the next level in your work or business.

In my first book *Moving On and Moving Up*, I addressed the issues we would face as God moves us from one assignment to the next, from one sphere of influence or authority to the next, from one season to the next. That book has been a launching pad for many to shift into their new season. If you have not read that first book, I want to encourage you to do so. The principles in that first book will help you lay a strong foundation for transiting into your new season.

This second book will take you beyond making a transition, to actually taking ownership of and expanding your sphere of influence at your new level. Together, these two books will prepare you to navigate the many changes you will experience as you move on and move up into God's destiny for you. (You can order all my books online at **www. naomidowdy.com**)

I am asking God to speak to you as you read this book. I am asking God to remove the frustration inside you concerning your purpose in the marketplace, and particularly in business. I believe that God's Holy Spirit is going to speak so clearly to you that you will begin to jump up and down

Your calling to ministry is really right where you are — on the 'mountain' where God has placed you.

declaring, "I found it! I found it!" You will find that your calling to ministry is really right where you are — on the 'mountain' where God has placed you.

God, I release a sense of peace and joy in this new discovery, right now. Keep reading, friends, and allow the Holy Spirit to speak to you.

Give Me This Mountain!

To appreciate and understand what God is doing today and where He is leading us, we need to understand how our concept of work, business and the marketplace has evolved through the centuries. Join me on a quick tour of history to get a glimpse of what God has done in times past, and what He is doing today.

- During the Dark Ages, the idea of church — and how church works — became really messed up. A distorted theology about clergy and laity emerged, creating a separation between the sacred and the secular. According to this theology, the church and the marketplace are separate realms — and should stay separate. The two worlds should never converge. This thinking was definitely not in alignment with God's Word or His heart. In the mind of Jesus, there was no such separation.

- This same theology created a chasm between pastors and 'the rest of us'. To be called into the pastoral or church ministry was a 'higher calling' than other professions. This non-biblical thinking produced generations of people who believed that "Since I am not a pastor, I am not in 'ministry'. I am just a layperson. I am in my workplace to earn a living, but work is work, not 'ministry.'"

- Because of this wrong theology, Christians lost sight of God's high esteem for work. Marketplace believers were isolated and made to feel excluded from 'real' ministry involvement. They were like second-class believers and silent spectators when it came to doing work for God's Kingdom. They did not understand their high calling as a minister to the workplace. Satan used this lie to eliminate an entire army of disciples who were already positioned in the marketplace.

- Christians effectively retreated from the world, leaving a void that Satan had moved into and begun to dominate. They lamented that society was going from bad to worse, but they did nothing to change it. They stayed out of the arena, retreating further into their religious world, and shunned active involvement in society and any attempt to alter the deteriorating conditions.

- Then God began to break our mindsets regarding the separation of the sacred and the secular, and restore to His people a biblical perspective of work. We began to see that work was a godly activity, not something to be despised. God Himself engaged in work (Genesis 2:2-3). Work was part of God's original intention for humanity. Adam received his work assignment (to tend the garden) before the Fall took place (Genesis 2:15).

- As God began to break old mindsets, Christians began to experience a paradigm shift in their understanding. God's marketplace believers came to realise that work was a God-ordained calling and activity, and that marketplace believers were there to bring glory to God as they did their work and business — God's way.

Understanding Marketplace Ministry

Today, there are two streams of understanding regarding marketplace ministry. In the first concept, the marketplace is a place for evangelism. The '9 to 5 window' is a place for evangelism and ministry, as people in the marketplace can only be effectively reached by marketplace people whom God has already strategically placed there. Evangelism — not work — is the key purpose of our presence in the marketplace.

The second concept about marketplace ministry is that we must go beyond evangelism. While every Christian should be witnessing and sharing Christ wherever we go, marketplace ministry is more than just witnessing for Christ. The marketplace should also be a place in which we use our anointing to transform society and extend the Kingdom.

This requires a change in our thinking about what constitutes the Kingdom of God. The activity of God in our world is not confined within the four walls of a church building. The nature and scope of the Kingdom of God goes beyond 'church' as we traditionally define it. We must become convinced that God wants every believer to saturate and influence every sphere of society. This means:

- Contributing to society through the quality of our work

- Modeling Kingdom values through our integrity of character and how we relate to our co-workers
- Conducting our work and business according to Kingdom principles, and influencing the value systems of businesses and corporations, so they will begin to align themselves with the value system of the Kingdom of God
- Influencing and mentoring others through our network of relationships and partnerships
- Leading through Kingdom vision and strategies
- Bringing about change and transformation in society

Now, this does not mean that we will have heaven here on earth. However, we are called to be salt and light of the earth, and to bring impact and change wherever God places us – in our assigned place. That is the essence of transformation.

Reclaiming the Seven Mountains of Culture

In recent days, the concept of 'Reclaiming the Seven Mountains of Culture' has become a rallying cry for taking ownership of our specific assignment in the marketplace. This has gained momentum and is now bringing about a renewed sense of focus and impetus towards transforming society. To understand the concept, we need to go back to that original revelation.

In 1975, God simultaneously gave Bill Bright, founder of Campus Crusade, and Loren Cunningham, founder of Youth With a Mission, a message to give to the other. That message was: If we are to impact any nation for Jesus Christ, we would have to affect the seven spheres of society that are the pillars of any society.

In an interview with Kelle Ortiz and Os Hillman, Cunningham described how he received this message. Here is an edited transcript of that interview conducted in November 2007:

It was August, 1975. My family and I were up in a little cabin in Colorado. And the Lord had given me that day a list of things I had never thought about before. He said, "This is the way to reach America and nations for God. And [He said], "You have to see them like classrooms or like places that were already there, and go into them with those who are already working in those areas." And I call them 'mind-molders' or 'spheres'. I got the word 'spheres' from 2 Corinthians 10 where Paul speaks in the New American Standard about the "spheres" he had been called into. And with these spheres there were seven of them, and I'll get to those in a moment.

But it was a little later that day, the ranger came up, and he said, "There is a phone call for you back at the ranger's station." So I went back down, about 7 miles, and took the call. It was a mutual friend who said, "Bill Bright and Vonnette are in Colorado at the same time as you are. Would you and Darlene come over and meet with them? They would love to meet with you." So we flew over to Boulder on a private plane of a friend of ours. And as we came in and greeted each other [we were friends for quite a while], and I was reaching for my yellow paper that I had written on the day before. And he said, "Loren, I want to show you what God has shown me!" And it was virtually the same list that God had given me the day before. Three weeks later, my wife Darlene had seen Dr. Francis Schaeffer on TV and he had the same list! And so I realized that this was for the body of Christ.

I gave it for the first time in Hamburg, Germany at the big cathedral there to a group of hundreds of young people that had gathered at that time. And I said, "These are the areas that you can go into as missionaries. Here they are:

- First, it's the institution set up by God first, the **family**.

- After the family was **church**, or the people of God.

- The third was the area of school, or **education**.

- The fourth was **media**, public communication, in all forms, printed and electronic.

- The fifth was what I call 'celebration', **the arts, entertainment, and sports**, where you celebrate within a culture.

- The sixth would be the whole area of the economy, which starts with innovations in science and technology, productivity, sales, and service. The whole area we often call it **business** but we leave out sometimes the scientific part, which actually raises the wealth of the world. Anything new, like making sand into chips for a microchip, that increases wealth in the world. And then of course prediction sales and service helps to spread the wealth.

- And so the last was the area of **government**. Now government, the Bible shows in Isaiah 33 verse 22 that there are three branches of government, so it's all of the three branches: judicial, legislative, and executive."

Cunningham went on to say:

"And then there are subgroups under all of those seven groups. And there are literally thousands upon thousands of subgroups. But those seven can be considered like Caleb: "**Give me this mountain**," and they can be a 'mountain' to achieve for God… and we will see it as not just a job to get money to stay alive, but "as the Father sent Me, so send I you," Jesus said… If you're a lawyer in a legal office, you are sent of God… Or if you're in Hollywood, or you're working as a dentist, or you're working as a doctor, everything you can do for the glory of God.

You may be in the area of food services. The Bible says in Zechariah 14:20 that even the cooking pots will be called holy to the Lord. That's food services. Or transportation. Everything from a bus driver to an airplane pilot or to a car dealer or whatever it is, it says even the veils of horses will be called holy to the Lord. So we make whatever we do, if we do it as unto the Lord, a sanctified, or a holy work, it is holy unto the Lord. It's not just the pulpit on Sunday, that's one of the spheres. It's also all the other spheres together, and that's how we achieve advancing the kingdom of God.

You can read the full transcript of this interview at Os Hillman's website, www.reclaim7mountains.com

Where Do We Go From Here?

What will it take for God's people to reclaim the Seven Mountains of Culture? There are conferences and workshops being organized. This is good because it is creating great awareness, but we need more than just conferences. We need examples and models of how God can use us to bring about transformation in our assigned mountain. We need a practical action plan. That is what this book is about. Whichever mountain you are on, you will be able to apply these practical principles, and if you are on the Business mountain, you will find the insights especially relevant.

I believe that you long to fulfill God's purposes and desire to see His Kingdom come, His will be done on earth as it is in heaven. I want to give you some practical principles and handles so you can go beyond desire, move beyond discussion, and launch into practical action. Now is the time to grab hold of God's Word to you, and move on and move up to the next level.

I want to give you some practical principles and handles so you can go beyond desire, move beyond discussion, and launch into practical action.

CHAPTER 1

Embrace Your Divine Assignment

Have you ever struggled to identify where you fit into God's big plan? God has a divine assignment for each one of us. Most of us can function in many different areas, with varying degrees of success and satisfaction. Perhaps this is what you have been doing. But to move on and move up to the next level, you will need to know your divine assignment and embrace it.

To do that, you will first need to embrace your call to the marketplace. While many believers have settled this issue, some are still struggling with their call. They face a nagging sense of guilt about the 'pull' inside of them towards the marketplace.

I once met a man who was serving as a pastor. However, he could not get rid of this feeling that he should be doing business. He wrestled with this because as a pastor, he was not supposed to be doing business! Eventually, he felt so compelled that he resigned from pastoral ministry to go into business. He did well in business. Yet he was greatly criticised by his pastor friends and congregation because to them, he had 'backslidden'. In their eyes, he had left the 'holy calling' of pastoring and had now taken a 'lower' calling, that of being in the marketplace. But in reality, he had finally stepped into his real calling and assignment from God.

A marketplace assignment is not a second-class assignment. It is not a lesser calling. It is an equal calling. It is God's calling. That makes it a high calling. It is God's sovereign calling and placement for us. That is why I call it a divine assignment. The

A marketplace assignment is not a lesser calling. It is an equal calling. It is God's calling.

big question for you today is to examine your own thinking to see if you have remnants of the traditional mindset that 'only what we do within the church is for God'. Have you completely accepted that God's divine assignment for you is in the marketplace?

Do Not Despise Your Gift

Secondly, you need to value the gifting or anointing God has given you. We sometimes do not value and accept our gift; in fact, we may not think very much of it or may even despise it. Since 2001, I have had the privilege of mentoring someone in Indonesia whom God is using powerfully both in the church and the marketplace. Before she knew Christ, Indri Gautama was a very successful businesswoman who owned seven different companies. After she came to know Christ, she felt that God wanted her to serve Him. She could not see how her gifting, expertise and experience in the marketplace could have a part in her service to God. In her mind, living for God meant she had to get rid of her businesses, companies, cars, houses and assets.

That was exactly what she did. This was almost like taking a vow of poverty. She went to the remote places of Indonesia to live and preach. She did this for many years. Later, when God led her to start a church in the city, she still had the mindset that 'I will never go back into business. The business world is corrupt, the environment is not good, and I don't want to be a part of it.' But within three years of pioneering her church, she soon found herself in the position of needing to use, once again, her business anointing.

She had a vision of constructing a complex comprising a condominium, offices and auditorium facilities that would include facilities for her growing congregation. This was no ordinary church building project: it was a hybrid development comprising commercial facilities and residential properties that would be available for sale in the open market. It was a breakthrough concept that required her to link up and partner with land developers in the city. The project was also significant in that it created jobs and business opportunities for church members who would otherwise not have such opportunities.

In the process of securing land and linking up with these land developers, she was chosen by the other directors to be the chairperson of the entire project. As chairperson, she has maintained a high standard of integrity, honesty, openness and transparency. She operates with only one set of accounting books, which is a departure from the norm in that nation. This has impacted the business community, and has modeled to them that you can do business based on God's value system and

You can do business based on God's value system and still be successful.

still be successful. This has also greatly enhanced her ability to preach, teach and share Christ with business people who think the only way to succeed is to use unscrupulous methods adopted by many in the corporate world.

Today, Indri is functioning effectively both in the church and the marketplace. One role does not detract from the other. She is not neglecting her church responsibilities in order to do business. She is 100% a pastor and 100% a marketplace change agent. She has now committed herself to bring about transformation to other areas in the nation by her direct involvement in the marketplace. She has come to the place of valuing her gifting and marketplace calling. Have you?

Dual Anointing

There are many people who are functioning in both the church and marketplace, with plenty of evidence that God's anointing is upon them. In Trinity Christian Centre, Singapore, we have what we call 'bi-vocational pastors'. These are marketplace believers who have a dual calling — to be in the marketplace and to be a pastor in the church. It is not a temporary arrangement because the church cannot support them (as is sometimes the case in church planting situations), but because they are called to both arenas. Of course, we also have full-time pastors who are called primarily to lead in the church arena.

Now, you may wonder, does this mean that it is possible to be called to more than one mountain at the same time? Definitely! Sometimes we struggle because we are locked into a certain pattern of thinking. Your divine assignment does not have to be limited to one mountain. While the Seven Mountains provide a framework for you to identify and embrace your divine assignment, be careful not to apply it in a rigid manner that locks you into a limited sphere of influence. God may position you to impact more than one mountain. There are also possible areas of overlap across the mountains. For example, if you are in the field of education, you would be contributing to the Education mountain. But you could also be in education as a business. Thus you would be functioning on two mountains at the same time.

The key: Value your gift, and embrace the divine assignment God has given you. The important thing is to embrace what God has called you to do. If God has assigned you something to do, do it!

Know Your Mountain, Know Your Sphere

Thirdly, you need to identify and discern your specific assignment. Some of you may ask, "How then do I know God's divine assignment for me?" You get clues about your divine assignment from your anointing. If God has anointed you to create wealth, to communicate, to educate, or to govern, chances are that your divine assignment is in that area. That could be the mountain which God wants you to impact and change. God has work for you there.

You get clues about your divine assignment from your anointing.

It is important for you to know your mountain, as well as your assigned sphere on that mountain. I believe there are many spheres or subgroups on each mountain. No one person can impact all of the spheres on a mountain. Take the Media mountain for example. That is a big mountain with many spheres on that mountain. The Media mountain would include areas like movies, TV, the Internet, journalism, photography... the list goes on. The mountain is too big to be conquered by one person. Each person has been assigned or apportioned a sphere.

The Apostle Paul acknowledged that his divine assignment was to a certain sphere or portion on the Church mountain: "We, however, will not boast beyond proper limits, but will confine our boasting to *the field God has assigned to us*, a field that reaches even to you" (2 Corinthians 10:13, emphasis mine). What was his sphere or portion? In Galatians 2:7-9, he talks about his divine assignment to reach the Gentiles, while other apostles were assigned to reach the Jews. That was his sphere, and he labored and worked to reclaim that assigned sphere for God. In the same way, knowing your sphere frees you to focus on your divine assignment. So I challenge you: Seek God, ask for His revelation concerning your sphere and then go — take your mountain!

To help you identify if God's assignment for you is within a particular sphere of a mountain, you need to look honestly at your anointing, training, skills, and passion. Look at what motivates and excites you, and what you enjoy doing. What comes easily to you? These are all indicators of where God may be calling you to function. In his book *The Anointing: Yesterday, Today, Tomorrow* (Charisma House, 2003), R.T. Kendall describes the anointing this way: "The anointing is what comes easily. Your actual anointing is in operation when you function without fatigue. Your sphere of anointing is when you work without having to break a door down in order to walk through it… It comes easily — you can do it, and you know you can do it."

All this involves a process of discovery. Spend time talking to God and your spiritual advisors or mentors to glean collective wisdom before stepping out. Rarely do we see the end from the beginning. God's revelation is progressive in nature. Remember also that God has seasons for our lives. God moved David from a shepherd boy to a musician to a warrior and then to a king. Likewise, your current assignment may be a stepping stone to your ultimate assignment. When God moves you from one season to another, He will alter or enlarge your assignment. Your divine assignment is not cast in stone. God will move you from one level to the next.

God's ultimate assignment for David was for him to be king, but he was not ready at that time, so God had to bring him through a journey to prepare him for his ultimate assignment. Let me encourage you: Do not see the journey or the process as a waste of time. There is no such thing as wasted time in God. If you have been obedient to God, if you have been faithful to do "whatever your hand finds to do" (Ecclesiastes 9:10), you *will* come into that place of fulfillment and significance.

Divine Assignment, Divine Grace

When God calls you to move on and move up to a new level, you may feel that your divine assignment is beyond you. You may struggle with the magnitude of your divine assignment. The prospect of taking on the assignment may seem daunting or overwhelming. However, you can be

*Along with God's divine
assignment comes
the grace to fulfill it.*

assured that along with God's divine assignment comes the grace to fulfill it. God has given you the special 'grace' you need to fulfill your divine assignment: "But to each one of us grace has been given as Christ apportioned it" (Ephesians 4:7).

This grace that accompanies your divine assignment goes beyond gifting or even anointing. It is more than the ability to perform the task or function; it is divine grace released to you so that you are able to withstand and overcome the pressure and the opposition that come with your divine assignment. Consider this: Perhaps you can preach well, but God may not have given you the 'grace' to be a pastor. Let me say it another way: Some people may function well as team members, but they do not have the 'grace' to be the team leader. Conversely, if it is your divine assignment, you will experience the grace to weather the pressure and attacks that come along with such a role.

When you are graced to function in a certain sphere or area, you will find it easier, though not necessarily without its challenges. I have experienced this in my divine assignment. I have been a Kingdom road warrior for many years, making round-the-world trips that are essential for the fulfillment of my divine assignment. I am sometimes on the road for almost 8 weeks at a stretch. It is not uncommon for me to spend two whole days travelling on consecutive flights that go halfway around the world, frequently into different hemispheres. Often, I have to be 'up and about' and ready to preach almost immediately upon arrival. Such an intensive traveling schedule can be very tiring and draining.

Adjusting to different time zones poses a real challenge.

Ever so often, I am asked how I manage to do such extensive traveling. These questions frequently come from other traveling ministers (including those much younger than I am!) A typical query goes like this: "How can you do all the traveling you do? I take one short trip and I am wiped out for a month. Just how do you do it?" My answer is simple. By His grace! It is only possible because God has given me the needed grace to carry out my divine assignment. When God gave me those divine assignments on diverse continents, He also 'graced' me with the ability to travel extensively and not feel wiped out. I could not have done it otherwise.

When you embrace your divine assignment, you will notice that you have His grace to do what He is asking you to do. The heavy tasks become easy. The seemingly impossible tasks become possible. You may still get tired, but it does not wear you out. You may battle spiritual attacks, sickness and challenges – but you overcome them all and emerge victorious. That is why the Apostle Paul says in 2 Corinthians 12:9 that God's grace is sufficient! God *will* provide the divine grace you need to move on and move up to your next level — and succeed there.

Awaken the Giants

It is one thing to know your specific assignment; it is another to embrace it. Do you struggle with embracing your divine assignment for reasons you cannot quite explain? This could be happening because of the spiritual warfare that surrounds your divine assignment. Did you know the devil is afraid of marketplace believers and business people? He is afraid they will discover their God-anointed destiny in the marketplace. The devil is afraid, because this awakening will literally transform nations and economies. The devil wants to keep you from embracing your divine assignment. The devil fears

The devil fears the anointing and calling that marketplace believers have.

the anointing and calling that marketplace believers have, which, when fully realized, are capable of transforming cities to operational efficiency and of expanding God's Kingdom. (In another chapter, we will look at how to overcome the obstacles he puts in your way.)

The devil fears you because he knows who you are. Now it is time for *you* to realise who you are. Stop letting the devil defeat you. Begin to listen to the Holy Spirit right now. Invite Him to touch your heart and spirit regarding your high calling. Allow Him to show you how you may have undervalued your God-given gift. Invite Him to bring such clarity like never before.

When you are able to define and articulate what your divine assignment for this season is, you will gain a sense of purpose and clarity like never before. When you can bring an alignment between heaven (the giftings and callings God has placed in you) and earth (where you are and where you can function), you get into that assigned place from God. Work or business will no longer be a struggle or a burden. It will bring a sense of joy and fulfillment, and a deep peace that comes from knowing you are in the will of God.

Begin to arise and embrace your divine assignment.

Begin to let God stir up the anointing and awaken the dreams He has placed inside you. It is time to move on and move up.

Peak Points

Every marketplace Christian and business person must begin to ask themselves:

- What has God put into my hand?

- Why has God put me in the business I am in right now? Why am I here?

- What do I feel a stirring to do? What might my divine assignment be?

CHAPTER 2

Get a Kingdom Vision

Now that you have begun embracing your divine assignment, you must grasp God's purpose. To fully grasp God's purpose will require you to see your position in the marketplace or on your mountain as part of a larger Kingdom agenda.

Let's call it 'getting a Kingdom Vision'. When you view your role in the marketplace the way God intends, work or business suddenly becomes more than about making money. You begin to focus on how God will use you to extend His Kingdom.

God's intention is that you will be a blessing to your mountain, and extend His Kingdom in strategic ways. In Genesis 12:1-3, God told Abraham, "Leave your country, your people and your father's household and go to the land I will show you. I will make you into a great nation and I will bless you; I will make your name great, and you will be a blessing. I will bless those who bless you, and whoever curses you I will curse; and all peoples on earth will be blessed through you."

As believers in Jesus, we are all Abraham's seed and partakers of the Abrahamic covenant. Most of us already understand that we are included in Abraham's promised blessing. However, we must understand we are also included in the *purpose* of Abraham's blessings. God's purpose and blessing should not stop with us. We are blessed to be a blessing! You are to be a blessing to the mountain where God has placed you. Your company should be blessed because *you* are working there. Your presence there becomes a channel through which God blesses that company or organization. That can happen only when you focus on using the gift God has given you for your work and business.

God wants to bring about a paradigm shift in how you view your role in your company or organization. You are paving the way for God's Kingdom and God's system to replace Satan's rule on your mountain and beyond. You will strike fear in the heart of Satan when you begin to realize that you are not in the marketplace solely to make money. Rather, as you make money, God's purpose is added to your business, and your profits are for His glory.

You are paving the way for God's Kingdom and God's system to replace Satan's rule on your mountain and beyond.

Transformation Through Business

A few years ago, I met a businessman in Indonesia. He had a three-fold vision. First, he had a vision to provide a higher standard of English education in the nation. Second, he wanted to improve the standard of health care in the nation. Third, he desired to build schools and health clinics for the poor who lived in the remote areas and did not have access to these kinds of facilities.

He gathered business people, bankers and investors together and shared the vision with them. Working together, they were able to build a top-notch English university complete with carpets, air-conditioned classrooms, and teachers from America. This enabled students to receive an international education without needing to go overseas and be away from their families.

He then started a second category of schools. This next university conducted classes in the Indonesian language. Both of these universities were very successful. This entrepreneur used the profits from the first two universities to fulfill his third vision. He wanted to establish 1000 more schools in remote villages where the children had neither school nor teachers.

He and a group of business people then used the same concept to bring better health care to Indonesia. He established a top-notch hospital with top-notch doctors and facilities where patients paid the full price for their medical care. He used that to fund a hospital staffed by local doctors to help more people. Then the profits of those two projects were used to build medical clinics in regions where no modern health care facility existed. In each of the facilities, he also built rooms which churches could use to conduct services in that community. This was a tremendous blessing to many pastors. Now, friends, *that* is Kingdom vision!

Can you imagine the impact of a whole army of marketplace people consumed with a Kingdom vision and purpose, with practical strategies to bring about change and transformation in their city and nation? Where there is a Kingdom vision, there will be transformation in a village, a city… and progressively in a nation. We must get God's plan in order to see transformation happen through business channels.

When marketplace believers get a Kingdom vision, or when that vision gets hold of them, we will begin to see great breakthroughs:

- Entrepreneurs will receive revelation from God concerning business
- Prophetic intercessors will hear from God on behalf of companies and organisations
- New inventions will be created
- Covenant relationships will be formed between business people, and between business people and apostles and prophets
- New coalitions will be formed among Kingdom business people, so they can expand their businesses together
- Strategies will be birthed to create new jobs and develop economies that will turn villages, cities and then nations around
- Work groups for city and national transformation will emerge
- New alternative business plans will be developed that will change the economy in regions
- Signs and wonders in the marketplace will happen as God's Kingdom entrepreneurs and marketplace leaders birth something out of nothing.

What is your vision for the marketplace? What is your vision for your mountain? As you are reading this book, is God stirring something inside your spirit, nudging you to move on and move up to another level? Whatever your vision has been in the past, there is one thing I am sure of right now: You are receiving a bigger vision. Your faith is rising to a new level.

I can hear the Holy Spirit calling you to move your work and business to a new level.

- It cannot simply be about generating enough business to pay the bills and feed your family.
- It must be a growing, impacting, 'new wineskin' kind of business.
- You must expand your vision. God may be calling you to embrace a national vision or even a global vision that will impact and transform your mountain.

Shake off that small survival mentality for your life and marketplace ministry. Be bold and audacious like Caleb (Joshua 14:12). Ask largely: "Give me this mountain!"

Lessons From Nehemiah

If you read through the book of Nehemiah, you will see many valuable lessons that will give you a model for moving on and moving up in the marketplace. There is much we can learn from Nehemiah and how he fulfilled his divine assignment. Nehemiah received a divine assignment to rebuild the wall around Jerusalem. This assignment was not just about rebuilding a wall; it was about what that wall represented. If rebuilt, the wall would powerfully transform the city and the lives of the people in that city.

This is God's Kingdom intention for you and your work or business. There is no problem with making money; that is part and parcel of business. But Kingdom enterprise is more

God wants you to bring Kingdom transformation to the mountain of your divine assignment.

than just making money. It is about Kingdom transformation through every arena of the marketplace. God wants you to bring Kingdom transformation to the mountain of your divine assignment.

Keys to Receiving a Kingdom Vision

Could it be that you are even struggling with how to get a vision? Maybe you think you have heard from God but you are not sure. Or there may be something stirring inside of you but you have not been able to put words to it. Let's look at how Nehemiah received a Kingdom vision, and how you too can get a Kingdom vision.

1. We must have an ear to hear what the Spirit is saying. Nehemiah was a cupbearer in the palace when he heard about the conditions in Jerusalem. The walls were broken down and the people were afraid. The 'news bulletin' was like a wake-up call for him. No matter who we are, what title we have, all of us need to have an ear to hear what the Spirit is saying.

God always looks for a man or a woman who will hear His voice and take hold of His Kingdom vision. Likewise, we may hear, "Oil prices are going up. Business is bad. Corruption is rampant. People are afraid. The circumstances around us are getting worse and worse." But like Nehemiah, we need to hear it through the filter of God's Spirit. In other words, what is God saying to you as you hear about these circumstances?

When Nehemiah heard that the city was in ruins and the people were suffering, he aligned himself with God and the need. God stirred something in him. Nehemiah's response was to humble himself before God with fasting and prayer (1:4). In other words, Nehemiah immediately went to God. He took his burden and concern to God. He wept and prayed. As he did, God did something in him. It was the birthing and the beginning of a Kingdom vision that would eventually result in a monumental achievement: the rebuilding of the city wall in 52 days.

When you hear the voice of God, your first response must be to seek Him in prayer. God will begin to birth in you a Kingdom vision. You will begin to pray for your workplace or company. You will start to pray for your industry. You are going to cry out, "God, change the marketplace — and let the change start with me!"

2. We must have an eye to perceive a radically different future in God. Everyone living in Jerusalem could see the same problems Nehemiah heard about. However, they had been lulled into passivity. They accepted the circumstances as inevitable and unchangeable. The people had become comfortable with the circumstances. They lost their desire to attempt anything great for God. They lost the ability to dream and shape a different future for themselves and their families.

We too can become so complacent just doing, doing, doing the ordinary to survive, that our Kingdom vision for a radically different future is killed. Marketplace believers can become very comfortable in just subsisting and getting by. We reckon, "As long as I am 'getting by', why put in more effort in moving forward?" The chance of change seems too remote. We can live in a condition for so long that we become accustomed to it and accept it as the norm. Like the old song *Que Sera Sera*, we drift along thinking, "Whatever will be, will be…" That kind of thinking will kill God's vision for you.

But when God began to birth in Nehemiah a Kingdom vision, he suddenly gained a heavenly perspective on the situation. He began to perceive the possibilities in God. He began to be gripped by this vision of restoring and building something for God. Likewise, when God begins to birth a Kingdom vision in you, you will no longer be content with the status quo. You will begin to see what no one else sees. You will begin to perceive possibilities in God that are not yet evident to others.

> *You will begin to perceive possibilities in God that are not yet evident to others.*

Here is a paradox: God never changes, and yet God is always changing. He is the same, and yet He is doing new things. God wants to birth new inventions, new products and new business ideas through His people. It is a new season! There are marketplace people who — if they put their gift to work and hear from God — will be on the forefront of new waves of innovation, new trends in the economy, new business strategies.

Look beyond traditional avenues. Think out of the box. Consider how the humble telephone has evolved over the years. It became a mobile phone, and then they added calendar functions to it. Now you can even watch television on it! In God, you can begin to see these things and perceive new possibilities before others see them. That is the power of Kingdom vision.

3. We must have a hunger for change. As the result of a Kingdom vision, Nehemiah's hunger for God and for change became greater than his appetite for food. He began to hunger for a new reality. He began to set aside his usual routine to make room for the Kingdom vision that was growing within him. As the vision took hold of him, he wrestled with what role God might possibly want him to play in making it happen.

Often, we sit around and keep talking about the problem. We complain about the business climate but we don't take creative steps to change the situation. We complain and murmur about it, but we don't do anything to alter the situation. Business environments will continue to be unstable, manipulated by

We must dare to believe that what we hear on TV, and what we read in the newspapers, can change.

greed, driven by the values of the present world — until we dare to believe that what we hear on TV, and what we read in the newspapers, *can* change.

Who is going to change the marketplace? You are. God is sending you. He has anointed you, given you wisdom, experience, and all that you need to bring transformation. What more is it going to take? God wants to start a movement where every business person will rise up and declare, "God, use me to start a Kingdom revolution in the marketplace.

God, I dare to believe I can bring change."

The early church had no Internet or airplanes, and yet, as marketplace believers, they shared the gospel throughout the then-known world. They traveled and did business as they shared the message about God's Kingdom. How did they do it? The key — there was no dichotomy. They were advancing the Kingdom 24/7. It was holistic, not compartmentalized. Marketplace believers like Lydia the textile merchant (Acts 16:14) believed that they could do something, and they did.

Today, God wants to fill you with faith for the seemingly impossible. Dare to believe that change can happen. Dare to believe that restoration can take place. Dare to believe that blessings can be reaped. God wants to bring you to the place of having a Kingdom vision, a vision for impacting your mountain through your work or business.

The Price of Vision

To have such Kingdom vision is going to cost you something. Again, let's look at Nehemiah. To pursue a Kingdom vision took selflessness on Nehemiah's part. Nehemiah had to consider the things of God more important than his own agenda. Nehemiah was comfortable in the King's palace. If you are going to see change, you must be willing to get out of your comfort zone. Get out of your 'king's palace', whatever it might be. Nehemiah caught a Kingdom vision, and because of that, he was willing to move out of his comfort zone and run with his divine assignment.

How long will it be before you see change on your mountain? How long will it be till Christians in the marketplace arise with a Kingdom vision? I declare, now is the time! It's time to perceive the possibilities in God. It's time for a new movement of anointed men and women who will take their mountain for God.

Are you willing to pay the price to get a bigger Kingdom vision?

 **Peak Points**

- A vision is something inside of you. What's inside of you today? What do you see? What do you want God to do for you and through you?

- What do you need to do to align yourself with God? Nehemiah engaged in identificational repentance: "I confess the sins we Israelites, including myself and my father's house, have committed against You" (1:6b). In order to unlock heaven's blessings, you must bring an alignment between heaven and earth. Give your life, family and work or business to God. Get your life right with God. Get your household in order. When you obey God's commandments and decrees, He will fulfill His Word.

- What has God promised you? Nehemiah reminded God of His promises (1:8-9). It is okay to remind God of His promises! Begin to take hold of the promises of God for your work and business:

"God, You said You would take care of me. You said none of the weapons formed against me would prosper. You said You would go before me, You are behind me, You would never leave me or forsake me." God is faithful to keep His promises.

- What is it going to cost you to get a Kingdom vision?

CHAPTER 3

Expect Expansion

Once you get a Kingdom vision, you will no longer have a 'small' mentality. Your work or business will no longer be about simply getting by or just having enough to pay the bills or send your kids to school. You will begin to have an awareness of the greatness of God's plan for you. You will have a growing sense of expectation for expansion.

At this point, I want you to pray, "God, bless my work and my business so that I can have an influence for Your Kingdom." Go ahead, pray it! To some Christians, it may sound greedy and materialistic, when in fact, the opposite is true. If you pray, "God, give me sufficient money to survive, enough just to get by," you may sound humble, pious and religious, but it is actually a very selfish prayer because it reveals that you are only thinking of your own needs. God wants to supply over and above your needs so that you will have enough left over to sow into His Kingdom and to bless others.

For expansion to take place in your work and business, you must be convinced that God wants to prosper you.

1. **God wants to prosper you so that you can extend the**

Kingdom. It takes money to build and expand the Kingdom. It takes money to win people to Christ. It takes money to make disciples. It takes money to pay your staff, or to buy a bigger location for your business. With money, a business or ministry can travel, rent office space, buy advertising space, and the like.

2. **God wants to prosper you so that you will have greater influence.** People like to align themselves with winners. Successful businesses draw the attention of other people. When other people are attracted to you, you will begin to have a voice of influence. That's why it is important for us to have successful careers and businesses — not just for survival, but for expansion and growth. You are to increase your business, to expand your influence. When you have influence, you can invoke change.

Let me urge you to break that poverty mentality and pray the Jabez prayer: "Oh, that You would bless me and enlarge my territory" (1 Chronicles 4:10). This is why the previous chapters were critical for you to resolve in your spirit. Right now ask yourself, have you shifted your mindset concerning business? Can you embrace your marketplace calling as being from God? Can you now rise up and take new action steps to see your business expand and grow?

God knows your heart. What is the motivation of your heart: "God, bless me so that I can bless others" or "God, bless me so I can indulge in the finest things in life"? I believe you have begun to align the motivations of your heart with God's. That is why you should expect expansion and increase.

Use It — or Lose It!

Jesus taught over and over again that the Kingdom of God is something that should grow and multiply. I want to look at two parables that reveal this truth. These two parables are very similar, but their lessons are different. One is called the Parable of the Talents (Matthew 25:14-30) and the other, the Parable of the Pounds or Minas (Luke 19:11-27).

> *Jesus taught over and over again that the Kingdom of God is something that should grow and multiply.*

In the Parable of the Talents, the master gave three servants different amounts — five talents, two talents and one talent. One talent is equivalent to more than a thousand dollars. The two who were faithful to multiply their wealth received the same reward: "Well done, good and faithful servant! You have been faithful with a few things; I will put you in charge of many things. Come and share your master's happiness!" (Matthew 25:21, 23). Different amounts, same reward!

The Parable of the Talents demonstrates the importance of using the money or resources God has given you, whatever it may be. This teaches us to be faithful to use our different gifts or resources as God gives us opportunities. 1 Peter 4:10 tells us that "Each one should use whatever gift he has received to serve others, faithfully administering God's grace in its various forms." The key here is not how much ability you have, but how faithful you are to use what you have. The person with the least ability, if he is faithful to use it, will receive the same reward as the most gifted pastor, business person or leader you can think of.

One of the servants hid his talent in the ground. The master said to him, "You wicked, lazy servant!... you should have put my money on deposit with the bankers, so that when I returned I would have received it back with interest" (Matthew 25:26, 27). Do not neglect or hoard what God has given you! When Jesus comes, He will want to know what you have done with what He has given you.

Notice what the master did with that lazy servant's talent. "Take the talent from him and give it to the one who has the ten talents. For everyone who has will be given more, and he will have an abundance. Whoever does not have, even what he has will be taken from him" (Matthew 25:28, 29).

If you do not use what He has given you, God will take it away. That means if you hoard what you have, even the riches that you started out with will deteriorate and get

> *If you hoard what you have, even the riches that you started out with will deteriorate and get away from you.*

away from you. Some people have good jobs but they are always broke and in debt, because they are not properly managing the resources that God gave them.

You may protest, "Why did the master give it to the one who already has ten talents?" But at least the first servant did something with what he had. You could say that the master was doing a deliberate fund transfer. God likes to put His resources in good hands!

Now, perhaps you feel like that servant with the one talent. Maybe you feel that what you have is small and insignificant, incapable of much impact. It may just be your regular pay check. But what are you doing with what God has given you? Are you spending the whole thing or are you investing it so that it will produce gain? It may seem small at this moment, but God is testing you to see how you will handle the seemingly little that He puts in your hand. Remember, even the servant with the one miserable talent was expected to multiply it. He had to account not for what he had, but for what he did with whatever he had. Do something with what God has entrusted to you.

How Much Did You Gain?

The Parable of the Pounds or Minas is similar and yet different. Jesus told this parable because He was near Jerusalem and the people thought that the Kingdom of God was going to appear at once. He said: "A man of noble birth went to a distant country to have himself appointed king and then to return. So he called ten of his servants and gave them ten minas. 'Put this money to work,' he said, 'until I come back'" (Luke 19:12).

Each servant was given the same amount, with the same instruction: Work it. Invest it. Do business. Make money. Can it get any clearer than that? Jesus expects us to do business until He comes. He expects us not to hide our money or to use our business for pure survival, but to increase and multiply it.

Notice Luke 19:15: "He was made king, however, and returned home. Then he sent for the servants to whom he had given the money, in order to find out what they had gained with it."

Read that again. Did he come to find out how much they

It is not about the stewardship of money, but the creation of wealth.

had given away? No. He wanted to find out how much they had gained. The servants' task was not to simply watch over it. They were to use and multiply the resources entrusted to them. Thus we see the master returning to ask, "How much did you gain?" Jesus is not going to ask you simply to account for your resources. It is not about the stewardship of money, but the creation of wealth.

In faith, we are to use our gift to 'trade' (as it were) and bring profit to the Kingdom until Christ comes. The question then would be, are you using all the full privileges of the gospel — all the promises, all the power, all the anointing — that is your gift and your deposit as a believer?

You are the reservoir into which God has deposited them. When you put money in the bank, do you expect to just get the same amount back, or do you expect more? Wouldn't you at least expect interest? It is the same with Jesus. He has put a great deposit into you and expects you to grow and expand. He expects you to increase. He expects you to multiply, personally and in business.

In other words, our gifts and abilities may be different, but our job is essentially the same — use the gift! Use what He has given you, for great is your reward. Your reward is according to faithfulness and achievement.

The faithful servants were rewarded by being made rulers of various cities. The first servant who had gained ten more minas was put in charge of ten cities (Luke 19:17). You could say the reward for faithful work is always more work! Because of your faithfulness, God will trust you to manage cities. Not one city, but many cities. God's plan from the beginning was that you will rule and reign with Him. How is He preparing you for that assignment? By giving you an opportunity now to prove that you can handle your ultimate destiny.

Jesus has given you good and perfect gifts. He has put resources in your hands. Remember:

- God wants to prosper you.
- He expects you to use what you have to gain more.
- Great will be your reward.
- He is using your work and business to prepare you to rule and reign with Him.

────────◄ **Peak Points** ►────────

Are you convinced that God wants to prosper your work and business?

What has God put in your hand, and what have you done to bring increase to these resources?

How do you sense Him leading you to use and grow these resources in the coming days?

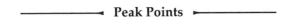

CHAPTER 4

Get Going!

It is great to have a Kingdom vision, but for the vision to become a reality, you will need to take concrete steps towards your desired destination or goal. God has promised to bless the work of your hands. Hands are symbolic of work, and work involves doing something. You must take action and do something. In other words, get going!

Let's take a look at the steps Nehemiah took to 'get going' in his Kingdom vision. Whichever mountain you are on, and whatever vision God has given you, these same steps would apply. Those who are called to the Business mountain will find these insights especially relevant.

Prayer

We have already seen that Nehemiah began with prayer. This is the beginning for all of us. Through prayer, Nehemiah heard God's voice, perceived possibilities that were yet unseen by others, and developed an intense hunger for a new reality. A Kingdom vision was birthed within him.

After he had prayed and discerned what role God might have for him in His plan, Nehemiah expected expansion. We know this because of what he prayed: "Give Your servant success today by granting him favour in the presence of this man" (Nehemiah 1:11b). This tells us that Nehemiah believed for favor and open doors.

As he came before the king, the king noticed the change in his countenance and enquired about him. Nehemiah told him about the deplorable state of the city. Then the king asked the million-dollar question: "What is it you want?" (Nehemiah 2:4) Now, how would you answer that question? Would you say, "Hmm... let me pray about that"?

So many times, when God opens the door of divine opportunity, we say that we need to pray about it. It sounds like the 'spiritual' thing to say! Notice that Nehemiah did not say, "Let me go fast and pray, and I will be back in 30 days." If he had done so, the king might have changed his mind about helping him! Prayer is wonderful. Prayer is needed. But Nehemiah had already done the major part of his praying — in the beginning.

Here was a *kairos* moment. Here was a door of opportunity. When a door of opportunity opens, that is not the time to pray and fast for 30 days. That's the time for action. That's why you pray and fast before. Nehemiah describes what he did when opportunity knocked: "I prayed to the God of heaven, and I answered the king" (Nehemiah 2:4b-5a). Nehemiah expected expansion. He was prayed up. He was ready with his answer for the king, and he received all that he asked for. He walked into the king's court with nothing, and left with all the resources he needed for his Kingdom vision.

As I interact with Christian business people in different countries, this is the point where I see so many of them falter.

There is that tendency to hesitate, pause, think about it again and procrastinate when it really is time to jump in and get going. This has resulted in many delayed or totally missed opportunities.

You need to be so in tune with God that when opportunity knocks, you can answer immediately. When the time of incredible favor comes, you need to be so prayed up that immediately you can pray, "Thank you, God, for favor" and then say to the king, "Here's what I need." Apostle Paul said, "Pray without ceasing" (1 Thessalonians 5:17). As you pray, be prepared. The answer to your prayer may come sooner than you think. You need to be so prayed up that when the door opens, you can walk right in and receive all the resources you need for your Kingdom vision. Your resources may come to you one piece at a time or all at once. The key is to be prepared.

You need to be so in tune with God that when opportunity knocks, you can answer immediately.

Preparation

Nehemiah knew that to start his Kingdom venture, there would be some basics that he would need, regardless of the circumstances he would face when he reached Jerusalem. There were three critical elements or areas of provision that Nehemiah had identified. Nehemiah asked the king for these three things:

- **Connections**
  Nehemiah asked the king for letters of introduction

(Nehemiah 2:7). One thing is for sure: If you are going to succeed in the marketplace, you will need divine connections. The success of a business depends on the success of others. If you want to produce a product, you will need someone to provide the raw material. You will need someone to transport it or to distribute it. Whether yours is a manufacturing company or a boutique, the principles are the same. You will need business connections.

It is important to trust God to connect you to the right people with the same vision and the same heart. It is also important that you involve other people. Give others an opportunity to walk with you in business and be blessed. This is a critical reason why marketplace believers need to network with one another, and attend workshops or mentoring sessions together. These are opportunities not only for personal growth and vision expansion, but also for networking with others in the marketplace.

I serve as the spiritual advisor to a group of business people who are doing this very thing. Global Business Network Partners (www.gbnv.com) is a group of Kingdom entrepreneurs who mentor and help one another succeed in business. At the same time they commit themselves to helping other people start new businesses or revamp existing businesses in order to achieve new levels of success and profitability.

- **Supplies**
The supplies Nehemiah needed were timber (Nehemiah 2:8). You may not need physical timber like Nehemiah

did, but you will certainly need other supplies, including human resources! You definitely need resources to start or grow a business or, if you are an employee, to enlarge your sphere of responsibility within a company or organization.

If yours is truly a Kingdom vision, you will not be able to fulfill it on your own. You will need to assemble a team. Pat Francis, a radiologist in Toronto, Canada, had an insatiable hunger for God, and served more and more in her local church. Later she felt called to birth a church and to be a pastor. At the

> *If yours is truly a Kingdom vision, you will not be able to fulfill it on your own. You will need to assemble a team.*

same time, God gave her a burden to help youth and people at risk. It soon became obvious that tithes and offerings alone could not fulfill the vision. By searching the Scriptures, she realized she had an entrepreneurial anointing for business. She knew it would take Kingdom entrepreneurs to create wealth to fund her Kingdom vision.

As she began to share her heart, vision and passion for God, the Lord sent her a team of entrepreneurs, strategists and talented business people. They began to create Kingdom enterprises with the mission to create wealth for Kingdom purposes. Pat says, "My business mission is prosperity with purpose and wealth creation for His cause." She and her team have created two main companies, Admarie Communications Services (www. admarie.com) and Elomax Enterprises (www.elomax.

com), each with several sub-companies.

No matter what your business is, or what industry you are in, the right supplies and resources are critical for the fulfillment of your vision. It is wisdom to seek help in a new venture. Do not be ashamed to ask for help from experienced people you know. An often overlooked area is staff. For example, you will need honest accountants. You will need good secretarial assistants. You will need legal advice. You must surround yourself with people who are committed to the vision and competent at the task at hand.

Supplies and resources for your business can come through normal channels or through newly opened doors as God expands your business network.

- **Protection**
  Nehemiah requested for the protection of the King's troops (Nehemiah 2:7). You too will need protection and covering in order to fulfill your Kingdom assignment. You and your work or business will need protection, both physically and spiritually. As you become God's Kingdom entrepreneur, you will definitely begin to experience spiritual warfare. This is not something to fear but it is something to be prepared for, so you will know how to engage and overcome in the spirit realm. I will discuss the importance and role of business intercessors in the next chapter.

When Nehemiah arrived in Jerusalem, he did further preparation. Now he could do what he could not do before;

he could survey the ground. He personally went to check out the situation (Nehemiah 2:11-15). Notice that Nehemiah did not stay in his prayer tower or executive suite. Nehemiah got personally involved. He got out to where the problem was. He not only prayed, but he went down to the ground where he was going to be working. He did an assessment and a study to determine just how bad the situation really was.

In other words, he took steps to complete a 'due diligence' before embarking on the venture. He did not rely on rumors or gossip. He went into the 'environment' where he was going to be working to check out the situation for himself. Likewise, in your Kingdom venture, you have to do your due diligence and your homework to ensure you are on the right track. You must know your market, know your competitors, and understand the challenges you will face.

When you are in the preparation stage and doing your due diligence, you will especially need to be interacting with your spiritual covering. If you do not have a spiritual covering or trained marketplace intercessors, you should seek them out. They should be a part of the process as you consider new business ventures. When you are sure you are ready to move on, you will need protection, especially in the spirit realm.

Presentation

All this while, the officials did not know where Nehemiah had gone or what he was planning (Nehemiah 2:16). Notice that he had not said anything to anyone as yet. He didn't start talking about the problem or the goal. Everyone could see the problem. But not everyone could see the solution.

For example, if Nehemiah said, "The walls are broken down. Let's rebuild the wall", they might say, "Well, the wall has been broken down for a long time. Nobody has ever rebuilt it before. I don't know if we have the resources." They would think of every reason why it could not be done!

There are people who have become so accustomed to their current situation. Even if you give them a new goal or vision, they will see it through the lens of old wineskin thinking. They will see it through the lens of the failures of the past. Everything you try to bring across will be misinterpreted or interpreted through the old mindsets. Does that sound like something you might have encountered in your work or business?

Too often business people have adapted to the prevailing conditions until they cannot see beyond them. For example, coffee is coffee, right? Wrong! Starbucks began to package and present that old familiar thing called coffee with new names, with a new look and served in a new setting. Once that barrier (mindset) was broken, suddenly there were many kinds of coffee being served in many new settings. For Nehemiah, the wall had never been rebuilt. For you, what is it that has never been done which God is nudging you to do? Don't wait. Be the first one to do it. To be first, you must jump in and just do it.

Nehemiah begins to cast vision for the future: "Come, let us rebuild the wall...and we will no longer be in disgrace" (Nehemiah 2:17). This includes both vision, and the reason for the vision. A critical element of vision-casting is communication. What we communicate and how we communicate can impact the reception of the vision. The vision must be powerfully presented. Vision-casting must take people from the known to the unknown. In vision casting, the first thing you want to do is remind people where we are and where God wants to take us. Begin with where they are and set a new future before them.

Vision-casting also clarifies the 'why'. Notice what Nehemiah told them "then we will no longer be in disgrace." That was the reason for the vision. It was not just to build a wall. It had much greater implications on the identity of God's people and the reputation of God Himself.

- *Why are we starting a new business?* God wants to bless us so we can be a bigger blessing than we have ever been in the past. Christian business people will no longer be seen as running small and insignificant businesses on the fringe of society. God wants to raise up powerful businesses that will be able to lead and shape transformation in the city and in the region.

  > *God wants to raise up powerful businesses that will be able to lead and shape transformation in the city and in the region.*

- *Why are we expanding our influence?* "So that we will no longer be in disgrace." We will no longer be a disgrace in arts and entertainment, business, education, government, and all the other spheres we talked about earlier.

- *Why are we going into a new market or region?* God wants us to create jobs for people, to bring people out of poverty and debt, and to bring Kingdom transformation to villages, towns and cities.

Proclamation

After Nehemiah presented the vision, the people caught the vision (Nehemiah 2:18b). They responded, "Let us start rebuilding!" When you cast the vision, and people catch that vision, the Holy Spirit verifies in their hearts, "Yes, this is from God." That is when the people become committed to the vision. They are now ready to 'get going' on the Kingdom venture. When the vision was 'caught', Nehemiah was able to boldly make a proclamation and declaration into the heavenlies against all of those who would oppose the plan and purposes of God. He thus established the purposes of God for the whole Kingdom venture of rebuilding the wall.

Keep talking, keep dreaming, and keep preparing. As you do so, you are promoting your vision.

When God gives you a vision to begin or expand a business, or to extend God's Kingdom on your assigned mountain, you need to share that vision. Talk about it — to the right people, of course. Keep talking, keep dreaming, and keep preparing. As you do so, you are promoting your vision.

Something that plagues many of us is procrastination. Have friends, intercessors and spiritual advisors around you who will keep pushing you to follow through with what God has put in your heart. They will also help you discern God's timing to launch your new venture. No more procrastination. Come on, it is time to get going — move up now!

 **Peak Points**

Suppose you sit down for coffee one day with someone who turns out to be a venture capitalist. He is all ready to invest in your Kingdom vision, and asks you what you need. What would your answer be?

What connections, supplies and protection do you need for your work and business?

Describe the 'what' and the 'why' of your Kingdom vision. Now practice communicating it and articulating it.

CHAPTER 5

Identify and Overcome Obstacles

How many of you know that when you start on a venture or enterprise, you are going to have problems? Those problems will keep you praying on your knees and will give you lots of tears, but you know there is victory ahead. Sometimes, the challenge comes in the most unexpected places.

After Nehemiah received a Kingdom vision and embarked on his assignment, he received opposition (Nehemiah 2:10). Now picture this in your mind. Nehemiah has secured the resources he needs for his Kingdom vision. He has cast the vision, and the people have caught it. They are all on board. He is feeling great about how things are going. But suddenly, here comes a threat. He might be thinking, "God, I am answering Your call. I am doing what You put in my heart. If You sent me here, why am I having this opposition?"

You can be sure that when you get going and move ahead with your Kingdom vision, you will receive opposition. Not everyone is going to understand you and God's new season for your life and your business. You will have your Sanballat, Tobiah and Geshem. These were the three men who opposed Nehemiah's Kingdom vision.

When they heard what Nehemiah was attempting to do, they were disturbed that someone had come to promote the welfare of the people and improve the circumstances. In other words, they did not want to see a Kingdom vision fulfilled. They did not want to see Kingdom transformation come to that sphere or area. Now, why would they be disturbed because someone wants to help? That kind of thinking can only come from Satan himself. It's a satanic spirit. The devil is out to steal, kill and destroy. Satan wants to destroy your vision. He wants to derail your progress. He wants to rob you of your prosperity. He wants you to become complacent. He will allow you to have enough to keep you happy, but not enough to have the ability to bring transformation.

As you rise up and take your rightful place in the business realm, you will discover that Satan will not want you to achieve more or become more influential. He will not want you to be successful in establishing a Kingdom business. Therefore you must be prepared to war for your inheritance.

See if you can identify with some of the obstacles that Nehemiah encountered. You may discover that some of your major obstacles fall into these same categories.

Ridicule

One of the first obstacles Nehemiah faced was ridicule (Nehemiah 2:19). God may be calling you, like Nehemiah, to establish something that has not been established before. It could be a new business model. It could be the enhancement of an existing product that God is leading you to repackage for today's market. People may mock and ridicule you because it has never been done before. Your new business idea may seem improbable. For instance, in the Middle East, near the city of Dubai, they have built a huge facility where you can snowboard and snow ski — right there in the desert. If you had heard of the idea, would you have found it laughable and ridiculous? Probably some skeptics did. Yet it has been successful in drawing tourists.

Likewise, ridicule could also come when you are attempting to birth new business opportunities in an area or region. If you were successful, it would release jobs and wealth for you and for the people, and profits for the Kingdom. Now that would really shake up the devil, because people would be breaking out of the bondage of poverty.

If you were successful, it would release jobs and wealth for you and for the people, and profits for the Kingdom.

Your new business may be established in a neglected area or among a neglected people. That would be something that would inspire many more people to rise up and see new possibilities for Kingdom transformation and expansion.

Fear

A second obstacle is the element of fear (Nehemiah 4:8, 10-14). Fear is something that can paralyze your faith. Fear can stop you from accomplishing your Kingdom vision.

Today, the hot topic on everyone's agenda is world shortages. There seems to be a shortage of fuel, a shortage of food and a shortage of water. There is an increased fear of famine. People are predicting that famine is coming to the world. There is power in the words that we say. These words have been released and are creating fear internationally. Governments and countries want to hoard their supplies.

Let me be bold to declare that this is a satanic influence to create crisis in the world. There is no dangerous shortage of oil, yet our prices continue to rise. There is no shortage of food; it is a distribution issue. There is no shortage of water; it is a management issue. There is no reason for the world to be in famine. "The earth is the Lord's, and everything in it" (Psalm 24:1). He has already given us "every seed-bearing plant on the face of the whole earth and every tree that has fruit with seed in it. They will be yours for food" (Genesis 1:29). When people fear hunger, the spirit of violence and self-preservation begins to dominate and take over. Now we have created an 'unreal' crisis.

Your enemies in the spirit realm will want to cause you to focus on what others might think about you, and thus cause you to hold back in fear. They will also want you to be afraid of what others may say your motives are. In some cases, your new business just might attract the attention of governments. Don't fear that. Welcome the opportunity to have governments ask for your input on how to bring transformation to villages, cities or even a nation. That fear does not come from God. So break off that spirit of

Break off that spirit of fear, and welcome God's Spirit of boldness, power and a sound mind into your life and business.

fear, in the name of Jesus. Welcome God's Spirit of boldness, power and a sound mind into your life and business. Rise up and move forward!

Intimidation

A third obstacle used against Nehemiah was intimidation (Nehemiah 4:3 and 6:14). Notice what they said of his Kingdom endeavor: "What they are building — if even a fox climbed up on it, he would break down their wall of stones!" (4:3). They tried to intimidate and demoralize Nehemiah.

Intimidation can come in the form of a challenge: "What do you think you are doing? Who do you think you are? What makes you think you are a marketplace leader? What makes you think you can change things around here?"

There is a spiritual enemy behind the intimidation, and the persons involved may not even know that they are being used by the devil. Sanballat, Tobiah and Geshem may have human faces, but

Sanballat, Tobiah and Geshem may have human faces, but there is a demonic spirit behind them.

there is a demonic spirit behind them. Recognize that you are not fighting against human flesh. It's a spiritual war. A spirit of intimidation comes to shut you down. When you are intimidated, you cannot plan with confidence, and you cannot speak with authority. Notice that this happened more than once. The enemy uses the same tactics over and over again. He thinks that the more he uses them, the more likely he is to wear you down and cause you to give up. You must refuse to be intimidated.

Challenging Your Integrity and Motives

The fourth obstacle will be a challenge to your integrity and motives (Nehemiah 6:5-7, 13). You start out in your work or business saying, "I will honor God. I will be a model for others." But at some point, you will be pressured to conform to the corrupt standards around you. People will tell you that the only way to prosper is to engage in corrupt practices. Those are the devil's ways, not God's ways. In many nations, corruption is rampant. Your business partners

People will tell you that the only way to prosper is to engage in corrupt practices.

will begin to feel the pressure, and they will put pressure on you. You are God's agent. You are God's instrument for change. What will you do then?

This is where the real test comes. Satan will hit you where it hurts you the most — in your wallet. The area of finances can create fear and paralyze you. The enemy will also want to create questions about your motives and integrity. He will want to increase the pressure on you until you begin to compromise and do business like everyone else. Satan wants you to do business with broken-down walls. He does not want you to become secure and grow. The enemy will want to stop anything — any plan, any cooperation — that will bring blessing and restoration to and through the marketplace.

War for Your Inheritance

Besides the four obstacles we have looked at, there can be

many other obstacles, including people, your own mindsets, blindness to opportunities, finances, family issues and a broken spirit, which can prevent you from trying new things.

In overcoming all obstacles, the primary battle will take place in your mind. Some of us have the idea that our thoughts are not that important. Thus we entertain or allow a lot of junk into our minds. Remember that your thoughts can create open doors or build huge obstacles that need to be overcome.

Do you realize that your thoughts actually possess dynamic power? Your mind is the battlefield for your soul. Therefore, if your enemy Satan can destroy or distort your thinking (about yourself or your business), he can cause you to become a failure. However, the good news is, God invites you to have the mind of Christ. That means you can have a renewed mind and begin to bring your thinking into alignment with God's Word. This step alone will propel you toward success.

I think we would all admit that our mental battles are the hardest battles to fight. Two key questions need to be answered: "Does everything really belong to the Lord? Is the earth really His and everything in it?" When you are convinced of the answer to

If God owns everything, then it is His good pleasure to give you the Kingdom.

these questions, you will have freedom to face and overcome every one of these obstacles. If God owns everything, then it is His good pleasure to give you the Kingdom (Luke 12:32).

Overcoming Obstacles

Let's look at how Nehemiah overcame the obstacles he faced.

- First, he declares faith: "The God of heaven will give us success" (Nehemiah 2:20a). You will succeed at what God has told you to do.

- Then he makes an apostolic declaration: "But as for you, you have no share in Jerusalem or any claim or historic right to it" (Nehemiah 2:20b). In other words, he cuts the opponents off from an inheritance in the victorious city that will be established. That is awesome authority. Do not misuse your authority, like James and John who wanted to call down fire from heaven. But you do have authority to cut things off in the spirit realm. You have a right to say "God, close the mouth of our enemy. Cut off those who oppose Your purposes."

If God has given you a Kingdom vision, know that the vision will be attacked. The battle is not about your work or business, but about all that it represents — the transformation of your assigned mountain. The marketplace is not merely a place for the expression of physical work. It is your spiritual assignment. If it is a spiritual battle, you will need spiritual weapons. Here I want to emphasize again the importance of prayer. We need to remind God of His Word:

If God has given you a Kingdom vision, know that the vision will be attacked.

"So is My word that goes out from My mouth: It will not return to Me empty, but will accomplish what I desire and achieve the purpose for which I sent it." (Isaiah 55:11)

Now is the time to move on and move up in your work and business. If God has declared that He will give you the land, then rise up and begin to take the land. You must adopt a warrior spirit. You must begin to rise up and call upon God, declaring, "You created me to conquer. Yes, there have been interruptions and obstacles. Yes, I have allowed obstacles and intruders to block me again and again. But now is the time for my inheritance!"

Will your path be without challenges? Of course not. But one way to look at your work or business is this: You are being paid to solve problems. This is why your prayer life is so critical. You must hear from God on how to solve each problem or challenge that comes your way. When you do this well, you will discover that many will seek out your counsel and wisdom for their work and business.

Apostolic Marketplace Intercessors

There is a new breed of apostolic intercessors who are specifically called and anointed to pray and intercede for people and businesses in the marketplace. A wonderful friend of mine, Tommi Femrite from Colorado Springs, Colorado, founded the Apostolic Intercessors Network (AIN) for this purpose. She and her team of intercessors war on behalf of multi-national corporations, as well as small and medium enterprises, and declare God's purposes and promises over these businesses. Here are a few testimonies Tommi shared concerning how God used them.

- Recently my wife had a dream that our ministry can only go as high and far as our intercessors can take us. This is why I called you. My testimony is that since I called you and obtained prayer from your intercession team, my business has been moving forward at the speed of light and I am seeing great success.

  - Director of an International Trading firm

- We saw an immediate increase in the area of finances after you interceded for us!

  - Dean of an Educational Institute

- Apostolic Intercessors Network is a very key part to keeping us Kingdom-aligned.

  - Owner & CEO of an IT firm

- Apostolic Intercessors Network has given me the 'momentum' to advance the Kingdom of God in my marketplace ministry and take dominion over one of the Seven Mountains in our nation.

  - Owner of a Financial Services firm

There is also a place for spiritual advisors and spiritual counsel. Personally, I am the spiritual advisor for a number of companies. I provide spiritual covering and counsel to these business owners. I journey with them and battle alongside them against such obstacles, and it is a joy for me to see them grow and prosper.

John Kelly, whom I know as a great friend and fellow apostolic strategist, is doing the same thing through

International Christian WealthBuilders Foundation (www. icwbf.com). John brings together Christian business people to learn how to do business at another level. He is right on the cutting edge with the annual 'Power to Get Wealth' conference where training and networking take place.

Business people need to have a prophetic edge, and they need a working relationship with an apostle and prophet. I believe we will see an increase of partnership in this area as God begins to increase our awareness and understanding of the spiritual dynamics involved in reclaiming the Seven Mountains of Culture.

Know Who You Are

To overcome obstacles, you must recognize the Sanballats, Tobiahs and Geshems. You must know how to handle them in your spirit. To do that, you have to know who you are. You must know that you have been called by God. You must be convinced you have been placed on your mountain by God. You have to stand your ground and say, "Nothing will intimidate me."

Nehemiah knew God had sent him. You need to be certain that God has put you in your workplace or business. Can you see why it was important for you to challenge and resolve some of the old mindsets about the marketplace? Can you understand why you needed to experience a divine shift in your own thinking? You may not even have recognized some of these as obstacles before, but now you must begin to identify and remove the obstacles before you. God wants to help you move on and move up, but you must overcome and conquer the obstacles.

You need to be prepared. Unexpected things can distract you. How do you stick to your God-given vision without being shaken? Stay focused. Nothing is impossible with God. Turn to God, and He will turn the situation around. Now it is time to move on and move up to the next level in your work or business, while slaying all the giants along your journey. Dare to believe.

God says, "Now faith is being sure of what we hope for and certain of what we do not see" (Hebrews 11:1). You must see through the eyes of faith what God has prepared. How do you get a glimpse of what God has prepared? As you pray and commune with God, God will begin to build that vision in your heart. You will see more than the natural eye can see. That is 'next level' faith.

◄ Peak Points ►

Which of the obstacles mentioned in this chapter have you been battling, perhaps without even realizing it?

What spiritual weapons are lacking in your current battle strategy?

What steps would you take to include these spiritual weapons in your arsenal?

CHAPTER 6

Take Risks and Seize Opportunities

There comes a time in your life or business when you must begin to step out of your safety zone. You either step out by faith or you will remain stuck in the old. I am talking about those times when you need to take risks and seize opportunities. Every time you expand, you take a risk. Every time you do something different, you take a risk. This is the only way you will move on and move up in your life.

This is the only way you will move on and move up in your life.

Too many times, we want to wait until we have every piece of data, every detail, a complete list of everything, before we begin to move. That kind of mindset will hinder you and cause you to miss divine opportunities that God may bring your way. Some of you will have opportunities to make mid-life career switches. That is a risk. In fact, you could say that Nehemiah made a huge career switch. He was making a transition from one career or industry into another. He was going to attempt something that he had never done before — construction and government.

Marketplace people must be risk-takers. You must be willing to step into the unknown. When God leads you into a new business or into a new area of expansion, He will not give you all the details. An entrepreneurial person does not need all the details. Once they have sufficient information and the assurance that God is leading them, they are willing to step out into the unknown. Pioneers take risks. They are men and women driven by a vision.

What do you need to know to move forward? You need to know that your new venture or opportunity is from God. Of course, you do your due diligence, and you still may not have all the answers, but you are in that place where God confirms, "Walk ye in it." That's when you step out of the boat. Peter could have said, "But I've never walked on water before." You may be saying, "I've never done this business before" or "I have never done business in this way before. I feel like I am in over my head." This is when your marketplace anointing begins to kick in. Business people with an entrepreneurial anointing are not bound by fear. They are willing to take risks. They are risk-takers, but they are not reckless.

The marketplace is a place where we will always face danger and opportunity at the same time. In the Chinese language, the phrase 'crisis' is a combination of two words — 'danger' and 'opportunity'. I love the lessons we can learn from these combined elements of danger and opportunity. It is so clear in Scripture. A great example is when Peter attempted to walk on water:

The marketplace is a place where we will always face danger and opportunity at the same time.

74

During the fourth watch of the night Jesus went out to them, walking on the lake. When the disciples saw Him walking on the lake, they were terrified. "It's a ghost," they said, and cried out in fear.

But Jesus immediately said to them: "Take courage! It is I. Don't be afraid."

"Lord, if it's You," Peter replied, "tell me to come to You on the water."

"Come," He said.

Then Peter got down out of the boat, walked on the water and came toward Jesus. But when he saw the wind, he was afraid and, beginning to sink, cried out, "Lord, save me!"

Immediately Jesus reached out His hand and caught him. "You of little faith," he said, "why did you doubt?"

And when they climbed into the boat, the wind died down. Then those who were in the boat worshiped Him, saying, "Truly you are the Son of God." (Matthew 14:25-33)

Let's look at the lessons we can learn from Peter's encounter with Jesus.

Risk Requires a Revelation of God's Presence

We must see God at all times and in every circumstance.

Have you heard me say this before? Of course you have, and I am saying it again. As you embark on your journey to take your assigned mountain for God, you must maintain a close personal relationship with Jesus. You must see Him as more than a business partner. You must be willing to say, "God, I give You my business — all of it. You are in charge." Then after you have given it over to Him, ask God to 'hire' you to run the business for Him.

So the first key component is to acknowledge God's presence in your business. Yours is a Kingdom business. It is more than a for-profit business; it is a Kingdom enterprise. Like the disciples in the boat, you in your work or business will experience storms. These are times when the economic outlook is confusing and uncertain, when everything looks bad, and there are signs of impending economic slowdown. These are risky times for a marketplace person. The question will always be: Can you see Jesus in the midst of the storm?

> *Yours is a Kingdom business. It is more than a for-profit business; it is a Kingdom enterprise.*

Storms — sluggish markets, rising business costs and recession — are always looming on the horizon. Though the circumstances may look bleak in the natural, can you see Jesus watching over you during these times? When you have a clear vision of Jesus, you have an awareness of His presence. When Moses had to take a risk and move to the next level, he wanted a revelation of God's presence (Exodus 33:15). In essence, he told God, "If You are not going with me, I am not going to move."

Risk is Part of the Journey

In the case of Peter, we see him challenged to rise to a new level of faith. He wanted to experience a new dimension of walking with Jesus — walking on water! He wanted to attempt something no other person in the fishing industry had done. It would require extraordinary faith. Jesus extended the invitation to him: "Come."

The other guys in the boat could have taunted him, "Hey Peter, you are taking a big risk, man. Don't be silly. Sit down. Don't rock the boat." When you attempt anything new for God in life or business, you must become a risk-taker. If you want to initiate change on your mountain, then risk is par for the course. When God wants to lead you into new things, He will always call you to go beyond your comfort zone. He will take you beyond your 'normal' limits. All of these elements can spell high risk in business.

If you want to initiate change on your mountain, then risk is par for the course.

There is risk when you get involved in God's Kingdom assignment. There is always risk involved when you start something new. There is a risk in loving people. There is risk in sharing the Gospel. There is risk when you try to bring about transformation. It is simply part of the adventure.

Risk May Imply There is No Model

No one had ever walked on the water before. If Peter had listened to his business friends who were all in the same boat with him, he might have never stepped out. The other guys could well have said, "Hey, Peter, be careful. Wait until someone else tries it first."

God told Moses to lead the Israelites out of bondage. Moses could have said, "Hey God, no one has ever led two and a half million people through the desert before. There is no model for this."

God told Joshua to march around the walls of that city called Jericho. Joshua could have said, "But God, no one has ever captured a city just by marching around it. There is absolutely no precedent for this kind of warfare."

God may want to give you new opportunities that He has never given anyone else before. Can you handle that? Many of the old methods of business do not work today. The world has changed. Methods of doing business have also changed. Now there is eBay, Amazon.com and so many other businesses that are purely Internet-based. You can shop for groceries online, or book your own holiday online without an agent. The list goes on. All these changes present opportunities for Kingdom entrepreneurs. Yes, there can be new dangers as you step into new opportunities. There may be no existing model for what God calls you to do. Will you dare trust God and say, "I will step out by faith, even if there is no model"?

It is time for you to allow God to stir in you the kind of deep passion that gripped David while he was still a shepherd boy. Others were paralyzed by the sight of a giant, but David could cry out, "Is there not a cause?" The answer is YES. There was no model for a giant-killer to follow. But David knew God was with him. He began to declare, "There is a cause" and he charged in. Listen, friends: God is with you. Believe it, take a risk, and slay your giants now.

Risk Requires Someone to Take the Lead

Here is a Kingdom principle: God will never do something new, unless He has found a leader to lead. The same principle is true in the marketplace. God can only work through someone who is willing to stand up and take the lead into the uncharted waters of a new invention, a new product or a new service.

There were many guys in the boat that day, all of whom were in the same industry, and yet only one person dared to stand up and take the lead. Only one had the faith to attempt the seemingly impossible. It was a test for Peter, and we can see that Peter passed the test.

The same is true for you. If God has given you a Kingdom vision, you must have that willingness to rise up and say, "God, here I am. I'm ready to move to another level of faith in business. I am willing to take a leading role in the new areas of business You are wanting to release."

Risk Will Involve Scary Moments

Anyone in the marketplace knows there are many things which can happen that can create scary moments for business people. The stock market is so unpredictable. Economies are no longer affected by their own national factors alone. We now live in a global village. Factor in all the natural disasters that are happening in various places, and we become keenly aware of the scary moments experienced by business people.

Peter took the step of faith to walk on water. But as he was coming toward Jesus, he saw how the wind was whipping up the waves. He began to fear for his life. He could feel himself beginning to sink. It was a scary moment! In that scary moment, Jesus reached out His hand and caught hold of Peter.

In the midst of scary, sinking moments in your mountain endeavor or in your business, have faith in God. He is with you. When you are in a high-risk situation, never be afraid or slow to pray. Peter's asking for help did not reflect on his capabilities. Asking for help is not a sign of weakness; it is a sign of wisdom. Cry out to God like Peter did. God will never fail you.

In Risk, God Will Give Us Victory

Peter had his scary moment, and it seemed like he had failed. Traditionally we have taken Jesus' question to Peter as a rebuke: "You of little faith... why did you doubt?" But I think it was just the opposite. I believe Jesus was saying to Peter, "You were doing great. You were walking just fine! What happened? Why did you doubt?" Jesus commended him and then taught him a valuable lesson in faith.

As Peter walked back with Jesus to the boat, the fact became clear that he was the first person in history ever to walk on water (other than Jesus). I can assure you, on that day, Peter moved to another level of faith. Peter walked back into the boat in victory, not defeat. Jesus will always pick you up and walk back with you in victory. There is always victory in Jesus!

One Window of Opportunity

In this entire account, there was only one window of opportunity. If you missed it, it was gone. Here, only Peter seized the *kairos* moment. Only Peter, out of all the others, experienced the presence of God in a powerful supernatural way. This was the window of opportunity that Jesus gave to all of His disciples. Only Peter seized the moment. You could get onto another boat on another day, but the circumstances would be different.

Many people can be doing business in the same community or in the same city, yet it might seem that only one is prospering. Why? God's eyes are running to and fro across the whole earth looking for an opportunity to bless His Kingdom business people. These are specific windows of opportunity. There are *kairos* moments to begin new businesses, and divine opportunities for you to expand your business like never before. Stay alert. Don't miss it!

I believe that God is going to open windows of opportunity for Kingdom entrepreneurs in the marketplace. Governments are going to seek you out for advice on how to alter the economic conditions in a city or nation. This is the moment when danger and opportunity come together for Kingdom purposes. This is the point at which your anointing and the needs of society converge to create a divine opportunity.

This is the moment when danger and opportunity come together for Kingdom purposes.

Now is the time for you to step out of your boat and

into God's new thing. Hear His voice. Begin to move in His direction. He will lead you. He will uphold you. He will be there with you. Will you recognize your divine moment in business? The choice is yours.

———————◄ **Peak Points** ►———————

What risks are involved in your divine assignment?

In what ways are these risks a convergence of both danger and opportunity?

What risks do you need to take in order to expand and extend your influence?

CHAPTER 7

Prepare to Manage Success

I believe God is going to prosper you and expand your influence in a greater measure than you have already experienced. But success can be a double-edged sword. It is a blessing and it can also be a curse. Sometimes success — and the money and recognition it brings — can corrupt a person. Therefore God will not bless you beyond what you are ready to handle. Hence, to move up to the next level, you must prepare for success. If you can manage success, God will trust you with more.

If you can manage success, God will trust you with more.

Can you see how critical this is to your continued effectiveness and ascent up your mountain? To ensure your future success, you must begin – right now – to build into your life and daily schedule the very things that will keep you grounded despite your marketplace success. This one factor can make or break you, and determine whether you can go from 'good' to 'great'.

When God's favor and blessings begin to pour in, watch out! You will be tempted to go out and spend all that extra money on a new and bigger house, a bigger car, or more expensive watches — status symbols that mark you as successful. You may even jump into expanding your business before you have secured the area where you are. Here is where the test will come. How well can you handle success? God is looking for Kingdom men and women who can handle

> *God is looking for Kingdom men and women who can handle major promotion and major increase.*

major promotion and major increase without becoming greedy, self-indulgent or puffed up with pride.

Success is a Double-Edged Sword

Business people are in business to make money. If that is your gift, you are to use it to create and multiply wealth. However, to become self-indulgent beyond reason would not be honoring to God. Always remember that you are blessed to be a blessing. It is not just to make you wealthy. It is much more than that. When you are faithful with the money God entrusts to you, you will not become a slave to it. Many people want money, thinking that money alone will solve all their problems. This is a delusion. Jesus Himself was emphatic about this: "No servant can serve two masters. Either he will hate the one and love the other, or he will be devoted to the one and despise the other. You cannot serve both God and Money" (Luke 16:13).

When you hear this statement, some of you will jump to the conclusion that rich people cannot serve God. But that is not what Jesus said. He said we cannot serve God and serve money. In other words, you can serve God and have money — as long as money serves you, and not the other way round. The important question is: Are you serving money, or is your money serving you? What relationship do you have with money? What power does your money have over you? The danger comes when you become a slave to money. This will stir up many other things within you which will show that you are not handling success very well.

You can become a victim of your own success. After you have experienced a measure of success, you may feel the pressure to replicate the sterling results again and again. If you are not walking closely with God, you will be tempted to step out and do it on your own without an awareness of His presence and a conscious reliance on His enablement. This can be very stressful, and the mounting pressure can overwhelm you and cause you to 'crash and burn'.

An immensely rich and hugely successful man of his time, King David, tells us in Psalm 62:10b, "Though your riches increase, do not set your heart on them." When we begin to set our heart on our riches,

When we begin to set our heart on our riches, our Kingdom vision can become corrupted and hijacked by self-serving ambition.

our Kingdom vision can become corrupted and hijacked by self-serving ambition. Our mountain endeavor becomes a pursuit of self-centered significance. Arrogance and pride can creep in and erode all the good that God has planned. It happens when, as the saying goes, a person begins to believe his or her own press reports. Pride is a deadly enemy and we must slay that giant every time it tries to raise its ugly head. Pull out your sword, the Word of God, and cut its head off. Be ruthless, for if you do not kill it, it will kill you.

People Power

When success comes, when recognition increases, and when your schedule begins to fill up with power lunches and other important meetings, it is easy to become self-important and lose sight of life's fundamentals. Your defense strategy against the corruption of success must include having people around you who will help you remain anchored and keep you from becoming big-headed about your achievements. These might be people whom you 'hung out' with before your present success, or people who have helped you get to your new level. They should be people who are not impressed by your success, and who will tell you if they see you going off-course. They will help you stay balanced and remain your friends regardless of your success or failure. "Wounds from a friend can be trusted" (Proverbs 27:6). Now, more than ever, you need such friends.

As I have mentioned earlier, spiritual covering and mentors are key components which help you hear from God and stay on track. You will definitely need a home church and pastoral covering. If you are not already in a church where you are growing spiritually, be sure to get into the life of a church. You will also need mentors and marketplace intercessors. Motivational speaker Mark Gorman has this to say about mentors: "A mentor is not someone who gives you advice. A mentor is someone whose advice you take." Based on this definition, how many mentors do you have?

> *A mentor is not someone who gives you advice. A mentor is someone whose advice you take.*

How to Stay on Track

To keep things in perspective, and keep your pride in check, you must use the same tools Jesus used when He was here on earth. Here are five spiritual components that had a great deal to do with how Jesus stayed focused and accomplished His divine assignment. If you are going to be a successful Kingdom entrepreneur, here are the spiritual components you need:

- *The Place of the Scriptures in His life.* Jesus studied the Word, quoted the Word, and used the Word in spiritual warfare with Satan during His forty days in the wilderness. Friends, if you do not read and study the Scriptures so that God can speak to you by His Holy Spirit, you will find that you have no weapons with which to fight your battles.

- *The Fullness of the Holy Spirit in His life.* The Apostle Paul said, "Be filled with the Spirit" (Ephesians 5:18b). The Holy Spirit is your guide. If you are not 'plugged' into Him as the source of power and revelation in your life, you will be vulnerable. This is because some things are only discerned in the Spirit, and not in the natural mind. Many times, people will tell you 'this is ok' or 'that is ok' — but they are not on the same page as you are when it comes to your business. They mean well, but they may not have the same values as you. They may not know what God is speaking to you personally, and it is what God is speaking to you privately that must ultimately be the deciding factor. Being continually 'plugged' into the Holy Spirit will protect you from wrong decisions.

- *The Power of Prayer in His life.* In the midst of the pressure and daily demands around Him, Jesus always took time to 'pull away' and pray. Prayer was a top priority with Him. Think about it: If Jesus needed to maintain a personal prayer life with God the Father, how much more must we prioritize our prayer time? You need to be prayed up in order to discern God's voice and know God's will in the many decisions you must make every day. If someone gives you a prophetic word, you need to take that word before God in prayer and judge that word in prayer. You must determine, with the help of the Holy Spirit, if you should act upon that word or not. Is it for you? Is it to be acted upon now, later or never? The only way to know the answer is to maintain a close and intimate relationship with God.

- *The Force of Faith in His life.* Jesus walked by faith in all He did. In all He did — whether He was driving out the demons, healing the sick, expounding the Scriptures, commanding the waves to be still, feeding the multitudes on two occasions, or raising the dead — He was operating in faith mode. He said, "I thank You that You have heard Me. I knew that You always hear Me…" (John 11:41b-42). Those are the words of someone who is walking in faith. We have already talked about taking risks and seizing opportunities. The only way to take risks and seize opportunities is by faith.

- *The Importance of Obedience in His life*. Before Jesus went to the cross, He had already wrestled in prayer at the Garden of Gethsemane (Mark 14:32-36). He prayed, "Yet not what I will, but what You will." He resolved in His heart to obey God and complete His God-given mission.

Your obedience must also be a matter of predetermination. Before the pressures and the challenges mount, you must determine what you would do and how you would handle them. You must make up your mind in advance and determine how you will conduct business — what you will do and will not do. Your predetermination will

> *You will need to determine, ahead of time, what your values and operating principles are.*

make a big difference in your business and in most of life's strenuous efforts. What kind of contracts would you accept? What kind of bonus or incentives would you pay to someone for their services? These are the many areas where you will need to determine, ahead of time, what your values and operating principles are going to be.

You cannot be indecisive or ambivalent. The Apostle James said, "A double-minded man [is] unstable in all he does" (James 1:8). It has been said that successful people are those who make decisions and do not waver, while those who are unsuccessful are slow to make decisions but fast to change them. Your predetermination is essential for your success and will also determine how you handle your success — by the world's values, or the ways of God.

You must pray, talk to your mentors and advisors, and then make up your mind to be steadfast for God.

These 5 components are the basic building blocks of your walk with God. Together, they form a hedge that will protect your current accomplishments and assets, and will ensure your future victory. If you faithfully incorporate these five elements into your life and schedule, they will serve you well in managing success. If any of these five elements is missing from your life, then take immediate action to get your priorities right. They will enable you, by God's grace, to navigate the circumstances without losing sight of the goal.

Keep the Faith

How would you know if you have been able to manage success? To the world, success means achieving a goal; to God's Kingdom people, success means achieving the goal while staying true to God's principles. There are some fundamentals to which we need to stay true. Here are 15 simple things we all know, but may not always remember to do. Most of this list is from Max Lucado's book, *A Gentle Thunder* (Thomas Nelson, 1995).

1. Be faithful to your spouse
2. Be a model for your children
3. Be the one who refuses to cheat
4. Be a good neighbor
5. Do your work without complaining
6. Pay your bills
7. Do not talk one way and then act another

8. Do a good job for others and for God
9. Be governed by proper ethics
10. Do not engage in gossip
11. Identify potential leaders and mentor them
12. Honor God in all your dealings
13. Do not attack another person's character
14. Do not break covenant relationships
15. Honor God in all your relationships

These may go against the grain of how things are done in your industry or company, or among your peers, but remember:

- You do not have to be like the world to impact the world.
- You do not have to be like the crowd to change the crowd.
- You do not have to lower yourself to their level — in order to lift them up to your level.

Finish Well

It is relatively easy to start well; it is much harder to finish well. Many men and women of God have failed midway in their divine assignment because of a failure to get a grip on success and the temptations it brings. Yet it is possible for you to succeed in the marketplace and stay true to God's principles. You can be like the righteous described in Proverbs 11:28: "Whoever trusts in his riches will fall, but the righteous will thrive like a green leaf."

In order for you to thrive and finish well, spiritual preparation is a critical part of your preparation. Never ever think — even for a moment — that because you are in the marketplace and not in the 'full-time' ministry (there's that old mindset again), you have no need for spiritual weapons. Wrong thinking!

We have already torn down the wall between the sacred and the secular. You are God's Kingdom entrepreneur, commissioned to bring Kingdom transformation to the mountain of your divine assignment. If you are to succeed in your Kingdom enterprise and your Kingdom endeavor, it will be by the grace of God. You need God to supply and grace you with the gifts, the resources, the divine connections and everything else you need to complete your divine assignment — and to finish well.

God's plan is to bless you and grant you success. The devil's scheme is to derail your progress and to destroy your credibility. Your greatest weapon against the enemy is to stay submerged in God's Word, sensitive to His Holy Spirit and surrendered to His will. Under His wings you will enjoy His protection and reap His benefits.

◄ **Peak Points** ►

Which of the 5 key components do you need to build into your life and schedule?

Which of the 15 simple things do you need to apply to your work and business?

CHAPTER 8

Go For the Double Portion

It is time to move from your 'survival' mentality and start thinking 'increase'. God wants to give you a double portion. God wants to erase debt, alleviate poverty and create wealth. God wants you to be the head and not the tail (Deuteronomy 28:13). Yet the fact of life is that "The rich rule over the poor, and the borrower is servant to the lender" (Proverbs 22:7). Therefore you must believe that God will break your poverty mentality, bring you out of lack and release you into abundance.

Poverty is Not the Will of God

The Apostle Paul reminds us in 2 Corinthians 9:8 that "God is able to make all grace abound to you, so that in all things at all times, having all that you need, you will abound in every good work." If you really take hold of God's Word and begin to declare, "God, You will supply all I need", this alone will empower you against Satan's attacks to rob and displace your business.

Deuteronomy 28 reinforces to me the fact that poverty is a curse. We discover that out of 68 verses, 14 verses describe blessings and 54 verses describe curses. From God's Word, we understand that the curse of the law includes spiritual death, sickness and poverty. Through the Abrahamic covenant we have the promise of blessings. Since the curse of the law is three-fold (poverty, sickness and spiritual death), it stands to reason that these curses must be broken.

- We know the curse of spiritual death is broken through salvation. When we receive Jesus Christ into our heart and come into right relationship with God, the curse of spiritual death is broken.

- What about sickness? Can this curse also be broken off our lives? 1 Peter 2:24 says, "He Himself bore our sins in His body on the tree, so that we might die to sins and live for righteousness; by His wounds you have been healed." What do we do when sickness attacks? We begin to claim our healing. We refuse to allow Satan to steal from us what Jesus paid a price to secure for us.

- What about the curse of poverty? Remember, Jesus came to reverse the curse — all of it. Thus our attitude toward poverty should be the same as it is about spiritual death and sickness. We must resist it and begin to declare that poverty is not the will of God for our lives and business.

You Will Lack Nothing

One of the keys to understanding that God wants you to prosper with His divine blessings is found in Deuteronomy 8:7-13:

For the LORD your God is bringing you into a good land — a land with streams and pools of water, with springs flowing in the valleys and hills; a land with wheat and barley, vines and fig trees, pomegranates, olive oil and honey; a land where bread will not be scarce and you will lack nothing; a land where the rocks are iron and you can dig copper out of the hills.

When you have eaten and are satisfied, praise the LORD your God for the good land He has given you. Be careful that you do not forget the LORD your God, failing to observe His commands, His laws and His decrees that I am giving you this day. Otherwise, *when you eat and are satisfied, when you build fine houses and settle down, and when your herds and flocks grow large and your silver and gold increase and all you have is multiplied...* (emphasis added)

We often read the rest of this passage without seeing the obvious picture that God is painting for us. We must begin to receive into our spirit the reality of what God wants to do. He wants to bless your finances. Read that verse again. It is a picture of absolute abundance, without lack or scarcity. Think of it this way: We

> *We must begin to receive into our spirit the reality of what God wants to do. It is a picture of absolute abundance, without lack or scarcity.*

are not like the Israelites in search of a Promised Land. We are a people who are living in a season of promises. The land is ours to take. Now enter in and possess the land!

Give Your Way out of Lack

One of the major keys to breaking out of poverty is to give your way out of poverty. You may say, that does not make sense. Yes, it may not make sense — but it works! No matter how hard it seems, just trust God and do it. I have seen this principle work in amazing ways.

When I first came to Trinity Christian Centre, Singapore, in 1975, they were a group with 42 members and 75 problems. Their chief worry was their inability to pay the bills. I told them, "If you have a financial problem, the way to get out of debt is to give. Give to God, and give to missions." At that first Missions Convention, we had faith promises amounting to S$30,000. The church owned no property. For years we rented halls, function rooms and public auditoriums for our worship services. We were like nomads moving from one meeting venue to another.

When I handed the church over to my successor Rev Dominic Yeo in 2005, the church had more than 4000 members and three properties in strategic locations — all freehold. When the current building project is completed, the total value of all three properties will be approximately $173 million. At this year's Missions Convention, our faith promises crossed the $9 million mark. We have moved from being nomads to being landowners! We have made the shift from searching for the Promised Land to possessing the Land.

People often ask me how it happened. Very simply, we taught what God's Word said about the principles (not just the promises) of faith and blessing. As we modeled it, people 'stepped out of their boat' and made faith promises — not according to their bank balances, but according to what they believed God was asking them to trust Him for. That broke the poverty mentality. People began to walk in the promises of God for their lives, career and business. Testimonies rolled in, and this encouraged others to believe God for the same thing. Now giving and faith are part of the culture of the church, and a hallmark of a Trinitarian.

The Miracle of Multiplication

God's principle is that of sowing and reaping. Galatians 6:7 says, "Do not be deceived: God cannot be mocked. A man reaps what he sows." When we sow a 'seed' offering into God's plans, He will multiply it. The principle works this way. On two occasions Jesus fed the multitudes. Each time, Jesus asked the disciples, "What do you have?" The first time, they showed Him five loaves and two fish (Mark 6:38). The second time, they gave Him seven loaves and a few small fish (Mark 8:5, 7). On each occasion, Jesus took the little that they had and blessed it. The blessing of God on the 'little thing' multiplied it, until there was much left over. The little became much. It multiplied until there was more than enough left over. It became more than a double portion!

Regardless of how small your business is, or how small and insignificant you may feel your position in the company is, God's blessing upon a seemingly small thing in an insignificant place will bring multiplication.

God's blessing upon a seemingly small thing in an insignificant place will bring multiplication.

God will multiply it until it is pressed down, running over and flowing over. It is time for multiplication, friends! It is time to give God the little thing you have — your business, your vision, your idea. Like the disciples, give what you have to Jesus. He will bless it, multiply it and bring increase. You are in the Kingdom of God, and the Kingdom has a creative anointing and a creative power. God will anoint you and give you inspired ideas on how to create and multiply wealth.

Prosperity in the Time of Famine

God's miracle of multiplication and blessing can happen at the most unlikely times and in the most unlikely places. An illustration of that would be in Genesis 26:2-3. There was a famine in the land, and yet "The LORD appeared to Isaac and said, "Do not go down to Egypt; live in the land where I tell you to live. Stay in this land for a while, and I will be with you and will bless you." God told Isaac to stay in a place of famine. Clearly that did not seem like a good plan but remember, it is always better to obey God. As we read further, we discover that Isaac planted crops in the land during the famine and the same year, he "reaped a hundredfold, because the Lord blessed him" (Genesis 26:12).

I know a businessman who owned a company that was doing well. Then the Lord told him to sell. He talked to his partners, but they were reluctant because business was so good. However, they finally agreed to go along with the man who heard God speak. They sold everything at a good price. Within four months, the whole market came crashing down. They were blessed because the man heard and obeyed God. I believe God protected the man because he was a faithful sower into the Kingdom.

If you have been faithful in sowing into God's Kingdom, God will release a double portion into your hands. You don't have to worry whether the stock markets are going up or down. Famine or no famine, God will prosper you.

If you have been faithful in sowing into God's Kingdom, God will release a double portion into your hands.

Possess the Land

I believe God's plan is for you to own your own home and, if you are in business, to own shops and businesses. Your business is part of God's plan to possess the land. Possess the land; take ownership of it. In Singapore, the government has a wonderful program that enables almost everyone to become a home-owner. That is powerful in our world today. However, I believe that God wants you to move from having a survival mentality of home-ownership to taking the position of a landowner. Let me add that God also wants you to move towards becoming the owner of many lands.

This will position you to inherit a double portion of blessing in the land. I am believing for Isaiah 61:7 to become a reality in your life and business: "Instead of their shame my people will receive a double portion, and instead of disgrace they will rejoice in their inheritance; and so they will inherit a double portion in their land, and everlasting joy will be theirs."

If you look at the lives of Elijah and Elisha, you will see a shift in thinking. Elisha did not just ask for Elijah's anointing or spirit; he asked for a double portion. You can do the same thing. Don't just ask for one business; believe for two or more. Don't just ask for one shop; believe for a franchise. Then ask for the nations as your inheritance. You have not because you ask not. When you begin to believe that God

When you begin to believe that God wants to bless you and move you up to another level, suddenly nothing is impossible.

wants to bless you and move you up to another level, suddenly nothing is impossible. No vision is too grand. No giant is too big.

Think Big

Let me challenge you to get a new mindset from God. God has positioned you for strategic influence in your city. He did not position you just for subsistence living. He has positioned you to hear His voice, so that you may dare to see yourself as an instrument in His hand for His glory. You are to impact the mountain where He has positioned you, so that the sphere you are in will begin to experience His transforming presence. This is the time for turnaround. God will begin with you. This is the time and this is the hour to say, "God, I trust you. Satan, you are a liar. Get behind me."

Do not say "I am just an employee" or "I am just running a small business". When Bill Gates birthed Microsoft, he was 'just' a student. Nehemiah, who was he? He was 'just' a cupbearer. The word 'just' reflects bad thinking. Get rid of the 'just'! God is calling you to function in the marketplace with new standards. Start a global business. Bring transformation.

Do things differently. Be among a new breed of Kingdom men and women who will rise up and release a new level of spiritual authority and anointing on the mountain of their divine assignment.

> *Be among a new breed of Kingdom men and women who will rise up and release a new level of spiritual authority and anointing on the mountain of their divine assignment.*

In 2 Corinthians 10:4, the Apostle Paul said, "The weapons we fight with are not the weapons of the world. On the contrary, they have divine power to demolish strongholds." The strongholds Paul referred to were the mindsets that prevented people of a city, a nation, or a culture from obeying and submitting to the truth of God. The same is true today. You need to move on and move up in business, to where you can assert your God-given authority in the marketplace and begin to introduce Kingdom transformation.

God has called you into the marketplace. I believe that He is now saying to you, "I have trained your hands. I have given you new ideas. I will open new doors for you. I have put everything you need within your hands." What are you waiting for? You must dare to believe in God and in yourself now. It is time for you to recognise your calling and anointing, and flourish in it — the way God has intended. It is time for you to rise up in your anointing. It is time for you to start impacting your marketplace. You cannot wait for someone else to begin transforming the mountain of your divine assignment. It must begin with you.

Today, begin to declare:

Get behind me Satan. I know who I am in God. I will stay focused on my calling and not be distracted. I will not be intimidated by man or religious systems or economic conditions, because the principles of God's Word do not change. I will go forward in what God wants me to do. I will be successful in the marketplace for the glory of God.

Friends, God will position you in ways you have never thought before. Dare to believe. Dare to step out of the boat. It is time to pack up, and come on up to a higher place. Move on and move up. Get going. I'll meet you again at your next level.

Is God calling you to move up
to the next level?
This book will help you get there!

*How I wish there were more Naomi Dowdys in the world!
If anyone is qualified to speak on the subject of moving to a higher
level in God, she is a prime candidate. This important book
will equip you in many practical ways to move to the next level
and to become the leader you were called to be.*
— J. Lee Grady, editor of Charisma magazine

Resources for Kingdom Entrepreneurs

**Divine Alignment for
Divine Assignment**

*Get aligned for your divine
assignment*

Declaration for Transformation

*Declare a shift into Kingdom
transformation!*

Taking Hold of God's Promises

*Positioning yourself so God's Word
will come to pass*

Kingdom Giving

The power of Kingdom investment

Get more of Naomi Dowdy's transformational teaching on
these audio CDs! Order them online at **www.naomidowdy.com**

Leadership Mentoring
with Dr Naomi Dowdy

For Business Owners, CEOs and Marketplace Leaders

Leadership is a lonely journey. Business leaders often find it difficult to talk to someone in confidence regarding issues in the business, their family or even their own lives. Christian business leaders find it doubly challenging, especially as they endeavor to integrate faith and business. Executive or life coaches are limited in their capacity to appreciate the issues faced by Christian business leaders, and the advice they give seldom aligns with the Word of God.

But now there is a platform where you can seek counsel from an experienced spiritual advisor and coach — Leadership Mentoring with Dr Naomi Dowdy.

About Dr Naomi Dowdy

Dr Naomi Dowdy is no stranger to entrepreneurship and business. Having founded and led several organizations of global impact, she has an in-depth understanding of the issues Christian business leaders face on a daily basis. Her spiritual counsel, leadership mentoring and apostolic covering have helped business owners and CEOs move up to the next level.

One-to-One Leadership Mentoring

This Leadership Mentoring will provide you with:

- A Leadership Mentor and Personal Coach who is committed to help you succeed in life and business.
- Apostolic covering, practical guidance and prophetic prayer support as you ride through the blips of business, and take the risks necessary to expand your business.
- A Spiritual Advisor who will journey with you and help you step into God's promises and destiny for your life.

- A Visionary Strategist who will provide input and inspiration for pioneering business models that combine profitability and Kingdom purposes.

These one-to-one Leadership Mentoring sessions will help you identify and help resolve issues in business, family and life. Confidentiality is strictly preserved.

Consulting and Speaking Engagements
Dr Naomi Dowdy is also available for:
- Consultation regarding the restructuring and realignment of organizations and companies
- Speaking engagements at events organized for business people, teaching on God's purposes so that business people can be established in their calling and embrace their role in Kingdom transformation.

Contact:
Dr Naomi Dowdy
USA: P.O. Box 703686, Dallas, Texas 75370
Singapore: Tanglin P.O.Box 48, Singapore 912402
Tel: (65) 6304-7766   Fax: (65) 6743-9608
Email: info@naomidowdy.com
Website: **www.naomidowdy.com**

Resources for Kingdom Entrepreneurs

Global Business Network Partners
www.gbnv.com

Global Business Network Partners (GBNP) is an independent Christian Marketplace Organization founded by Dr Naomi Dowdy, who also serves as its Spiritual Advisor and Leadership Mentor.

GBNP helps Christian business leaders succeed through:
- *Leadership Mentoring*, which helps CEOs and business owners to identify and resolve issues in business, family and life
- *Business Mentoring*, which helps business leaders to build godly values in their business and achieve business transformation.

The mentors at GBNP are experienced business persons, professionals, consultants and specialists with a proven track record of success.

GBNP also focuses on the establishment of sustainable business platforms to generate income for missions and social enterprises, and to create jobs in local communities, thereby leading to economic and social reforms.

Address: 346C King George's Avenue
King George Building, Singapore 208577
Tel: (65) 6222-3622 Fax: (65) 6221-5750
Email: info@gbnv.com

Apostolic Intercessors Network

www.ain-gki.org

Apostolic Intercessors Network (AIN), a division of GateKeepers International (GKI), is a cutting edge network that links apostolic intercessors with workplace leaders. AIN systematically provides prophetic intercession for apostles and other leaders in the workplace, thereby empowering them to strategically fulfill their destiny resulting in the transformation of society.

Workplace leaders and CEOs around the world are discovering the value of inviting the presence and power of God to work in and through their workplace by having personal and corporate intercessors for their business. Once these leaders have made the significant decision to invite and increase God's presence and power by submitting their business to intercession, finding or equipping those intercessors can be a challenge. AIN rises to that challenge to assist these leaders identify and develop intercessory prayer teams for their business.

Address: P.O. Box 1026,Wallis, TX 77485-1026
Tel: 979-533-4767   Fax: 979-478-6586
Email: info@ain-gki.org

International Christian WealthBuilders Foundation
www.icwbf.com

International Christian WealthBuilders Foundation is a partnership program established by Christian WealthBuilders and educators to advance the Kingdom of God. It is founded and led by John Kelly. Its vision is to empower an alliance of Christian WealthBuilders and WealthDistributors for the advancement of the Kingdom of God.

It is designed to offer many important keys to your future success. This program is not a 'get rich quick' tool, but an ongoing training ground of advanced learning to help you develop your maximum potential as a wealth generator and knowledge as a WealthDistributor. Its training is grounded on the Word of God.

Address: P.O. Box 820067, Ft. Worth, TX 76180
    Tel: (817) 232-5815 Fax: (817) 232-1290
    Email: ICWBFinfo@icwbf.com

Elomax Enterprises
www.elomax.com

The vision of Elomax Enterprises is to revolutionize the financial and commodity trading industries by creating a 21st century template that will manage a full range of transactions varying in complexity both locally and internationally. Elomax delivers a comprehensive range of financial services for people seeking a home, commercial property, looking for investment opportunities to earn more equity and create wealth, or to acquire commodities.

The President and CEO of Elomax Enterprises, Dr Pat Francis, has been appointed as a United Nations Representative with influence as a Transformational Activist to deal with humanitarian issues and systemic poverty in partnership with world leaders.

Address: 14-1224 Dundas Street East
Mississauga, Ontario CANADA L4Y 4A2
Tel: 905-566-2866   Fax: 905-281-9185
Email: info@elomax.com